MOUNTAIN
OF THE
DEAD

Keith McCloskey

MOUNTAIN
OF THE
DEAD

THE DYATLOV PASS
INCIDENT

In memory of

Igor Dyatlov
Lyudmila Dubinina
Zinaida Kolmogorova
Rustem Slobodin
George Krivonischenko

Alexander Kolevatov
Semyon Zolotarev
Nicolai Thibeaux-Brignolle
Yury Doroshenko
Yury Yudin

For Moira, Lucy, Callum and Jack

Front Cover. Top: The Dyatlov group well wrapped up against the elements.
Courtesy Dyatlov Memorial Foundation; Bottom: Naked woman. *iStockphoto*
Back Cover. The last photograph taken of the Dyatlov group while they
were still alive. *Courtesy Dyatlov Memorial Foundation*

First published 2013

The History Press
The Mill, Brimscombe Port
Stroud, Gloucestershire, GL5 2QG
www.thehistorypress.co.uk

Reprinted 2015, 2017

© Keith McCloskey, 2013

The right of Keith McCloskey to be identified as the Author
of this work has been asserted in accordance with the
Copyright, Designs and Patents Act 1988.

British Library Cataloguing in Publication Data.
A catalogue record for this book is available from the British Library.

ISBN 978 0 7524 9148 6

Typesetting and origination by The History Press
Printed in Great Britain by TJ Books Ltd, Padstow, Cornwall

Contents

Foreword

In February 2013 it was fifty-four years since the Dyatlov tragedy, which took place in the northern Ural Mountains. In what appears to be coming to prominence as the Russian equivalent of the *Mary Celeste* mystery, numerous theories have been put forward to try and explain what happened, but it appears to be a case that almost defies rational explanation. These theories, which try to explain what happened on the night of 1/2 February 1959, range from the quite plausible to what some may think of as the absolutely ridiculous. I have included them all (at least the known theories at the time of writing, including one that surfaced while I was well into the preparation of the book). It is important to keep an open mind and it is also worth considering that the cause of the deaths may involve more than one theory or a combination of theories.

The core of the mystery is not so much how the various members of the party died, but what caused them to flee from the safety of their tent in what appears to have been blind panic, fearing for their lives. There is also another line of thinking, which suggests that the deaths occurred elsewhere and their bodies were deposited on the slopes of Kholat Syakhl (Mountain of the Dead). The real problem is that there is very little evidence to go on, everything is conjecture. Also, part of the problem in finding an answer is the nature of the former Soviet Union with its mania for secrecy and security. Despite the fall of the former USSR, the opening up of archives and a different outlook among the younger generation, old attitudes still persist in many areas of officialdom.

I have also tried to give an idea of the background in which the tragedy took place. In other words, the Cold War, which dominated everyone's lives in the East and West at that time. I have also given a brief explanation of the part that 'ski tourism' played in the Soviet Union.

The only thing certain is that nine young people in the prime of their lives died dreadful deaths and, like the *Mary Celeste*, it is probable that the truth of what actually happened will never be known for sure.

Acknowledgements

First and foremost I am grateful to Christopher Jeffery for making the whole project possible as a fair amount of finance for research in the Russian Federation was required. Equally the book would not have been possible without the considerable input from Yury Kuntsevich, Chairman of the Dyatlov Memorial Foundation in Ekaterinburg. Running parallel with Yury's help was the excellent help and translating carried out for me by Marina Yakhontova. Marina is a first-class translator and is also extremely knowledgeable on the whole Dyatlov Pass story. Her kind assistance and help both during my research in Russia and 'over the ether' is deeply appreciated.

I am also grateful to: Alexander Gulikov via the Dyatlov Memorial Foundation for permission to include a condensed version of his theory 'A Fight in the Higher Echelons of Power'; Yury Yakimov for permission to include his 'Light Set' theory, which is a condensed translation of an article that first appeared on www.Russia-paranormal.org. My thanks goes also to Gillian McGregor and Peter J. Bedford (HM Coroner for Berkshire); Natalia Elfimova for her patience and help; Dr Milton Garces PhD; Michael Holm; Dr Gabor Szekely; Pavel Ivanchenko; the director of the Museum at URFU (formerly UPI), Julia Borisovna Shaton, and the curator, Irina Alexandrovna Kashina, who were very helpful and pleasant during our visit; Paul Stonehill and Philip Mantle; Galina Kohlwek; Olga Skorikova and my editor at The History Press, Lindsey Smith.

Special mentions also for: the last surviving member of the Dyatlov group, the now late Yury Yudin, who clarified certain grey areas and answered a number of what must have appeared mind-numbing questions during my research; Leah Monahan for her technical wizardry and unfailing cheerful patience; Triona McCloskey for proofreading. A special thank you to my wife Moira for all her help and unflagging support.

Finally, the British Consulate in Ekaterinburg for the best cup of tea east of the Urals.

Notes on the text

* In many articles and publications the word 'tourism' is mentioned and the Dyatlov group are referred to as 'tourists' or 'sports tourists'. This was a loosely defined term and a condensed definition of it in 1969 was: 'Tourism includes journeys with the aim of active rest and better health and performing socially useful work. An important part of tourist activity is moving around on foot, skis, bicycle or boat and overcoming natural obstacles often in extremely difficult climatic conditions and even in dangerous situations, e.g. mountaineering or rock climbing ... Many tourist journeys involve self-service, such as arranging a camp, camp-fire, food and washing. Sporting tourism also includes mountaineering and orienteering. The All-Union Sports Classification details the complexity of routes, the number of journeys, the length of the journeys and the difficulty of natural obstacles that the tourist has to negotiate in order to gain a ranking.'

G.D. Kharabuga, *Teoriya I metodika fizicheskoi kul'tury* (Moscow 1969)

* 41st Kvartal – (meaning 'quarter' or 'square') kvartal in forestry is part of a forest area defined by artificial fire breaks or natural terrain features such as rivers. Kvartals are an important element in cadastres, mapping, economics and forestry management. Kvartals may be of different sizes e.g. 4x4km, 8x8km or larger depending on the size of the forest. Kvartals are numbered in a direction from NW to SE. Quarter poles at lane crossings have numbers on their sides also oriented in the NW and SE directions. Rangers, geologists and tourists use them to find their locations on maps. The 41st Kvartal referred to in the text is a woodcutter settlement in the 41st Forest Kvartal.

★ Kholat Syakhl – strictly means 'Dead Mountain' in Mansi but, with the deaths that have taken place there, it has come to be known as 'Mountain of the Dead'.

★ Taiga – used to describe the Boreal Forest. The Taiga is also a biome or ecosystem that consists mainly of coniferous forests and covers a vast area in northern Russia.

★ Gulag – the acronym (in Russian – *Glavnoe uplavrenie lagerei*, meaning Main Camp Administration) for the system of prison camps across the USSR used to incarcerate criminal and political prisoners who were used as slave labour.

★ Names – wherever possible I have avoided use of the traditional Russian patronymic and used simplified first names in order to make reading easier.

★ Yekaterinburg/Ekaterinburg – there is not enough space to go into the various reasons why there are two different spellings for the city: I have chosen Ekaterinburg. Between 1924 and 1991 the city was named Sverdlovsk.

★ Oblast – government administrative region.

★ Mansi – tribe of the northern Urals region.

★ Khanty – tribe of the northern Urals, related to the Mansi.

Prologue

In January 1959 ten students from Ural Polytechnic Institute in Sverdlovsk set out on what they hoped would be an exciting journey and a test of their skills in the remote northern Ural Mountains, nearly 400 miles north of the city where they lived and studied. Although it was mid-winter and the conditions would be harsh, the trip was to be a break from the hard daily routine of their studies. The leader of the group was Igor Dyatlov who had only just turned 23, an affable and highly experienced skier, hiker and orienteer. There were two strong-willed girls in the group: Lyudmila Dubinina and Zinaida Kolmogorova. There were also another seven males: Yury Yudin; Rustem Slobodin; Semyon Zolotarev, a tough Second World War veteran and expert in unarmed combat; Alexander Kolevatov; George Krivonischenko; Yury Doroshenko; and Nicolai Thibeaux-Brignolle, who was born in one of Stalin's Gulags where his father, a French communist, had been imprisoned and executed.

The whole group were all very fit, experienced hikers and skiers. Only the previous year, Igor Dyatlov had led a party on the same route, so they were confident that there would be no problems encountered that they could not deal with.

They left Sverdlovsk and travelled north by train, lorry and then finally on foot and skis. On 27 January they reached an abandoned village of wooden houses, which had previously been used by geologists. They spent the night there and it was here on the following day (28 January) that one member of the group, Yury Yudin, decided to turn back because of illness.

Their target was to reach the 1,234m Mount Otorten (translated as 'don't go there' in the local Mansi language), but they ended up on the slopes of the 1,079m mountain named Kholat Syakhl (translated as 'Mountain of the Dead' in the local Mansi language).

Up until 28 January 1959, everything can be independently verified about the journey of the Dyatlov group. Beyond that date, and despite the presence of a group diary and photographs, nothing can be verified.

1

Journey to the Mountain of the Dead

The events leading up to and the night of 1/2 February 1959 have been reconstructed, as far as possible, from what was found by the search parties and the last entry in the Dyatlov group's diary for 31 January 1959, which was made by Igor Dyatlov. This chapter is also a reconstruction of what happened from the official point of view.

On 23 January 1959, the group of ten skiers spent the day in Room 531 at Ural Polytechnic Institute (UPI) in Sverdlovsk. They were all members of the UPI Sports Club and were frantically packing their rucksacks and getting their equipment ready as they had a train to catch. Assisted by the *zavchoz*, the university's head of provision distribution, they packed items including oatmeal, 3kg of salt, knives, felt boots and all the other accessories necessary for the journey.[1] The talk was on a very superficial level and, despite their anticipation of a journey they were all looking forward to, tempers were starting to fray. Zina Kolmogorova expressed her frustration at not being able to pack a spring balance. Rustem Slobodin asked whether or not he would be able to play his mandolin on the train – to which Zina sharply replied, 'Of course!' They considered the mandolin to be one of the most important pieces of equipment for the journey, as it would be their main source of entertainment. Luda Dubinina counted the money they had pooled together. Money was tight. They had been given 1,000 rubles by the Trade Union Committee at the university but they had to put in their own money as well. They were in high spirits and looking forward to their expedition, despite the last minute rush to ensure everything was packed and that they had not forgotten any food or equipment. That day, 23 January, was the first day on which an entry was made in the group's diary and in which they took turns to make the entries for the period of the expedition. The first entry was made by Zina; she wrote that she wondered what awaited them on the trip – although at that time she could have had no inkling of what was to happen.[2]

Their planned route was by rail to the town of Ivdel, via Serov, and then a bus would take them directly north to a small settlement at Vizhay on the River Auspia. From Vizhay the group would proceed on a hired truck, then on foot and skis, to Mount Otorten. The whole route from Sverdlovsk to Mount Otorten, with the intermediate stops, was more or less directly north–south and approximately 340 miles (550km) as the crow flies. From departure to their arrival back in Sverdlovsk, the trip was expected to take twenty-two days.

At this stage another person was expected to join the group, Nicolai Popov, nicknamed 'the morose fellow', who had agreed with the group leader Igor Dyatlov to provide his own supplies and equipment. Popov had already graduated from the university and was not a student. Fortunately for him he missed the train.

The group set out by rail from the main railway station in Sverdlovsk for the 201-mile (324km) journey north to the town of Serov. The young men in the group made a solemn promise to the two girls that they would not smoke for the entire trip. Zina doubted very much that they would have the willpower to keep their promise for so long. Once the train set off on the long journey north, they settled into their seats and Rustem Slobodin took out his mandolin. Together they sang songs they knew and composed new ones. Semyon Zolotarev was not well known to everyone in the group, but he fitted in quickly as he had a vast store of songs, many of which the students had never heard before. Because of his much greater experience of life, particularly as a front-line soldier in the Second Word War, as well as having been a Komsomol (Soviet youth organisation) leader, he was duly accorded respect by the others. Much has been speculated about Zolotarev who, like the story of what happened to the group, in many ways remains an enigma.

As they sang along to the the mandolin, darkness descended as the train continued its long journey north. They looked out of the window at the seemingly never-ending Taiga, which spread to the Ural Mountains on the left and on the other side to the vast empty spaces of Siberia. As well as the occasional appearance of a small severny (settlement), they passed several military bases (or areas related to the military) between Sverdlovsk and Serov. During the Nazi attack on the USSR in the Great Patriotic War (1941–45) – as the Second World War was known to the Russians – much of the military production (e.g. tanks and aircraft) was pulled back to the east of the Urals, far away from the Nazi advance and out of the range of Nazi bombers. With the advent of the Cold War, most of these facilities remained where they were, with expansion taking place and the addition of facilities to take account of the new atomic age. There was a major plutonium-producing complex at Kyshtym between Sverdlovsk and Chelyabinsk, which lay in the opposite direction (south) to which the Dyatlov group were travelling.[3] The Kyshtym plant was where George Krivonischenko had been involved in the clean-up after the 1958 nuclear accident. There were other facilities more or less on the route north on the group's line of travel. These included a gaseous diffusion production plant for plutonium U-235 at Verkh Neyvinsk to the north of Sverdlovsk,[4] and a large facility for the production and storage of nuclear warheads at Nizhnyaya Tura.[5] Travel in these areas was severely restricted and the presence of so many nuclear, military and associated facilities has a bearing on some of the theories relating to what happened to the Dyatlov group.

By 3 a.m. on the morning of 24 January, having exhausted their stock of songs and being exhausted themselves, Zina recorded in the diary that the rest of them had all fallen asleep as she surveyed the darkness outside the train window.

After leaving Sverdlovsk well behind them, the train pulled into the town of Serov at 7 a.m. on 24 January. Both Zina and Luda mention that they had travelled with another group of hikers from the university, led by Yury Blinov, who had left at the same time as them. Luda had suspected that Zina was keen on a male member of the Blinov group, as she (Zina) appeared upset when the two groups later split up. The two groups were well known to each other and Igor Dyatlov had given his radio set to the other group. However, upon their arrival at Serov, the reception the station staff gave them caused all feelings of empathy and friendship to disappear. As, despite the eary hour, they were not allowed in to the station building. In the diary, Zina described somewhat sarcastically the response from the staff as 'Hospitality'. A policeman had stared suspiciously at the group and they must have felt intimidated, as Zina further noted in the diary that they had not broken or violated any law under communism. The atmosphere of intimidation must have begun to annoy George Krivonischenko as he started singing, which was enough for the policeman to grab him and haul him away. The police told the group that Section 3 (of local railway regulations) forbade all activity that would 'disturb the peace of passengers'. Again Zina made a diary entry, which stated that Serov must be the only station where songs were forbidden. Eventually George Krivonischenko was released and the matter was settled amicably. Whilst it is possible to read something into the behaviour of the police towards the group, it is more likely that the group were boisterous and in good spirits in the early stages of their journey, which attracted the attention of provincial officers with too much time on their hands. Furthermore, the group had passed through an area containing sensitive military establishments and were starting to approach another area (around Ivdel) that contained numerous prison camps. In these circumstances, and at that time in a state obsessed by security, strangers automatically brought suspicion on themselves by their very presence.

Serov was more or less halfway from Sverdlovsk to Ivdel. The group had more than eleven hours to kill before they could take the next train to Ivdel, which left Serov at 6.30 p.m. They were warmly welcomed at a school close to Serov railway station. A janitor (*zavchoz*) heated water for them and made arrangements so that they could store their equipment. It was a free day for the group and the diary entry for that day was made by Yury Yudin. Yudin had wanted to visit a natural history museum or a local factory. Visiting a local factory may seem an odd choice as a way to pass the time but it was very much in keeping with the ideal of the young communist Yudin, who, although studying at a higher institute of learning, would still wish to express his solidarity with the factory workers and would have been welcomed by them.

However, much to Yudin's disappointment, the first part of their day was spent in checking their equipment and going through their drills and training. At 12 p.m. when the first part of the school day was over, the group organised a meeting with the schoolchildren. The meeting was held in a small cramped room where the children listened silently as Zolotarev explained what sports tourism was, and what they were doing on their trip. The children were possibly a little apprehensive of Zolotarev, but when Zina started talking they became more animated. She spoke to them individually, asking their names and where they were from, and was a firm favourite with the children as they asked her endless questions in return. After two hours, the children did not want the group to leave. They wanted to know each minute detail about the trip, from how the torches worked to how the tent was set up. Eventually the time came for the group to gather their equipment and make their way to the station for the train to Ivdel. The whole school went to the station to see them off. The children were upset at the group's departure, with some of them in tears and many of them asking Zina not to leave and to stay with them. Zina asked the children to make sure that they behaved well and studied hard. However, despite the emotional farewell, the group's problems with railway stations and the police had not ended. A young alcoholic accused someone in the group of stealing his wallet, with the result that the police were called. Luckily nothing came of it and the group were allowed to proceed without any further restrictions, much to their relief.

The journey by train to Ivdel was five and a half hours long. They settled down to talk (Zina proposed a discussion on the nature of love) and again to sing songs, accompanied by Rustem Slobodin's mandolin. Some members of the group used the time to revise for their exams. Their sustenance on this part of the journey consisted of garlic bread without water. The town of Ivdel was the last major point of contact with civilisation before they set out on the journey north into the more remote Siberian Taiga and the mountains of the northern Urals. The town itself was the centre of the Gulag camp system for the area. At one point there were almost 100 camps and associated subcamps of varying sizes in the vicinity of Ivdel. The town is situated on the Ivdel River near the confluence of the Lozva River, 332 miles (535km) north of Sverdlovsk. It had been the first wooden fortress east of the Urals, built in 1589, and became a gold-mining settlement in 1831. The first Gulag was established there in 1937 and eventually the population grew to between 15,000 and 20,000 inhabitants, a figure which has remained fairly constant.[6] Many prisoners who were released from the nearby camps decided to stay in the town as they had nowhere else to go. The same applied to the prison staff. A number of former staff who had finished working at the camps also decided to settle in Ivdel for the same reason – that they were familiar with the area and had nowhere else to go. The result was that, by 1959, a large segment of Ivdel's population was a strange mixture of former guards and the formerly guarded.

On arrival just after midnight on the night of 24/25 January the group alighted at Ivdel railway station. They found a large waiting room where they stored all their equipment and took turns to keep watch while they awaited the bus for Vizhay early the following morning: Sunday 25 January 1959. A comment made in the group diary by Yury Yudin is noteworthy: that they had 'total freedom of action' at the station at Ivdel. This was no doubt a reference to their two unfortunate previous encounters with the police at Serov station.

On their arrival at Ivdel, the group were 90 miles (145km) from Mount Otorten. After the short wait they took a bus to Vizhay where they arrived at 2 p.m. They decided to spend the night of 25/26 January in Vizhay before proceeding to the next point. Their accommodation was described by George Krivonischenko as a 'so-called' hotel, which must have been very basic even by the standards of the austere Soviet Union in the 1950s. There were not enough beds for the ten members of the group so they slept two to a bed, with both Sasha (Alexander Kolevatov) and Krivoy (George Krivonischenko) gallantly sleeping on the floor. Despite the inadequate accommodation, they slept well and rose at 9 a.m. on 26 January, only to find that the outside temperature was -17°C and a small window had been left open during the night, forcing them to get out of bed in freezing conditions. They relied on the hotel for breakfast and were given goulash and tea. Igor Dyatlov made a comment about the lack of heating in the 'so-called hotel', joking that if their tea was cold they could always go outside the hotel and it would soon warm up enough for them to drink it! They then arranged to get to the next point on their journey, the 41st Kvartal (this was a camp for geologists and workers in the area), by road in an open flat-bed type GAZ-63 truck that was organised to take them. A photograph of eight of the group shows them all sitting on the back of the open truck with wooden slatted sides exposed to the elements. Yet they were all well wrapped up against the wind and cold and again seemed in good spirits. The truck eventually left Vizhay at 1.10 p.m. on 26 January. Despite their layers of clothing the group were freezing on the three-hour journey and tried to occupy themselves by singing and animatedly discussing various topics, which ranged from love (a favourite topic of Zina's) to the nature of friendship and the problems of finding a cure for cancer. The bitter cold on the truck affected Yury Yudin badly and despite trying to hide under a makeshift tent they had made to keep off the wind, he developed a chill with lumbago and an acute pain in the leg.

At the 41st Kvartal they were glad to be able to get off the truck. Even though it was a remote area, there was a hostel there, which was operated with a dormitory system for the geologists and workers in the area to stay. However, the group were given their own private room probably due to deference to their status as educated students.

Whilst there they spoke to the workers and in particular befriended an older man called Ognev who made quite an impression on George Krivonischenko.[7] Ognev also made an impression on Luda who was keeping her own private diary (apart from the group diary that everyone had access to), in which she gave a fuller description of Ognev. On arrival at the hostel they cooked lunch and then rested. Films were available to watch in the hostel and some of them watched a film while the others occupied themselves individually. Rustem played his mandolin while talking to Nicolai. Krivonischenko spent his time checking the equipment to make any necessary adjustments to the packing. Krivonischenko had made the diary entry describing their arrival at the hostel and how they spent their time on 26 January, but there is a single cryptic comment in the diary for that day made by Nicolai Thibeaux-Brignolle in which he states: 'I can't although I tried.'

There is no further detail and no later comment regarding this single-line entry, but Nicolai is thought to be possibly referring to having started smoking again despite the solemn promise made by himself and the other males in the group that they would not smoke for the entire trip.

The next day, 27 January, the diary entry described the weather as 'good'. The wind was behind them and they reached an agreement with locals at the 41st Kvartal for a horse and a guide to take them to the next point on their journey (an abandoned settlement), which was approximately 15 miles (24km) further on. While waiting for the use of the horse they helped a local by the name of Slava (described as 'Grandfather Slava') to unload hay from a carriage. Some of the boys rewrote a song and then started singing with some of the locals and workers. One man in particular was described as singing beautifully. A number of forbidden songs were also sung, but these only by the workers,[8] as the comment in the group diary was 'We heard ...' rather than any reference to any of the group singing the songs themselves or joining in. Nevertheless, they obviously knew that the songs were illegal as they used the term 'illegal' to describe them. It is possible they either joined in or sang some themselves, but would have made no written reference to having done so for fear of possible censure if anyone in authority read their diary on their return. A further comment was also made in the diary regarding these songs as 'Article 58 Counter-Revolutionary Crimes'.[9]

The group departed from the 41st Kvartal at 4 p.m. on 27 January, with this 15-mile (24km) section of the journey on foot made much easier by having the horse pull their packs and equipment on a cart. Before departing they had bought loaves of soft warm bread and ate two of them on the journey. The second severny (settlement) they reached was abandoned and derelict, but Ognev had told Igor Dyatlov where they could find a habitable dwelling to settle for the night to break their journey.

It was at some time during this fifth day (27 January) of their journey that Yury Yudin's illness worsened. He had fallen ill on the truck travelling from Vizhay to the 41st Kvartal but had decided to tough it out and continued with the group as far as the second severny, as he wanted to collect some geology samples and then return to Sverdlovsk. The pain in his leg was getting worse and it had become apparent that he would be unable to meet the more physical demands of the rest of the journey in the mountains. He was diagnosed eventually with acute radiculitis. The second severny, which as mentioned was now abandoned, had been a settlement used by Soviet geologists while they carried out research locally. Yury Yudin was an economist but had an interest in geology and, despite his illness, he obviously felt there was some value in continuing with the group in order to search out samples around the settlement to take back with him to the university.

The horse pulling the group's backpacks and equipment moved slowly, yet the group was able to travel faster than if they had been carrying the stuff themselves. Despite complaints about the slowness of the horse, they covered 4 miles (8km) in two hours, reaching the River Ushma. By now, darkness was falling. Some members of the group had moved on ahead to reach the abandoned settlement before darkness fell completely. They wanted to find the house described to them by Ognev as it was the only place suitable to rest for the night as all the other buildings were in a bad state of disrepair, with a number of them literally falling apart. In the event, they managed to find the house described by Ognev in the complete darkness, out of the twenty-five houses in the settlement, and started a fire to keep warm. Several of them pierced their hands on old nails in the wood as they were gathering it for the fire. The horse and cart, with Yury Yudin sitting on top in order to spare his leg pain, along with the remaining members of the group, eventually arrived at the abandoned settlement later that evening. Once they had settled in, they sat by the fire and talked and sang until 3 a.m. the following morning (28 January) before going to sleep.

The first two members of the group to awaken on 28 January were George Krivonischenko and Alexander Kolevatov, who then woke the others. The weather was good, with clear visibility. Although the temperature was

-8°C, it was not excessively cold for the time of year and the area. After they had eaten breakfast, Luda made adjustments to the mountings on her skis and Yury Yudin went outside into the area near the settlement to see if he could find any minerals. There was nothing of any interest to him apart from pyrite and quartz veins in the immediate surrounding area. It must have been a relatively cursory search as he was to leave the group that day and return to Sverdlovsk on account of his illness. He possibly felt too ill to search properly, but at least would be able to show on his return that he had made an effort despite being unwell. Again, this display of stoicism would have fitted in well with the ideal of the young communist – who is prepared to do what is expected of him or her, no matter what troubles may have to be faced.

The first part of the diary entry for this day (28 January) was made by Luda, who was obviously very fond of Yury Yudin and sorry to see him go. Luda states that it was a pity ('especially for me and Zina') that Yury Yudin had to return. Luda appears to have been more demure than Zina. One photo shows Luda embracing Yury Yudin in a genuine display of affection for him before he leaves, while another shows Zina touching Yudin's face as a gesture of affection just as he is preparing to make his departure. After leaving his companions behind, Yury Yudin would dwell for the remainder of his life on what happened to them and how fortunate he was to have escaped their fate.

Once Yudin had taken his leave, the remaining members of the group set out on what is described as the first day of their journey proper. By this it is meant the actual part of the journey out into the mountains on their skis, out into the wild terrain and away from any civilisation. It was an area that was well known by Mansi hunters but there were no signs of habitation or any settlements.

Although the first part of the diary entry for 28 January had been made by Luda at the abandoned settlement, the second entry for that day was made by Nicolai Thibeaux-Brignolle, who describes the journey into the mountains from the abandoned settlement.

They went along and up close to the River Lozva (there are numerous rivers in the area, all relatively close to each other). Each of the remaining members of the group took turns to be in the lead for ten minutes at a time. Mention is made by Nicolai about the depth of snow being significantly less as compared with the previous year, which implies he had been there in 1958, possibly with other members of the group. This part of their journey was hard going as they constantly had to stop and wipe melted snow from their skis. George Krivonischenko was at the rear of the group making sketches of the route and terrain. They passed some small cliffs on the right bank of the River Lozva and then the terrain became flatter. At 5.30 p.m. on 28 January they stopped to camp for the first night. The tent they had was a large one that had been 'customised' by Igor Dyatlov and his friend, Boris Slobtsov. It was big enough to sleep all nine of them (it would have accommodated eleven in fact, had Yury Yudin continued his journey with the group and had Nicolai Popov also made the trip), and the interior had curtains with which to make compartments and also afford some privacy to Zina and Luda. Igor had built a stove that could be placed inside the front entrance, with the chimney going out of the tent and upwards at a right angle. The stove presented some problems while they assembled it; eventually they left some parts unassembled while they cooked dinner. After they finished eating, they sat around a campfire alternately talking and singing, accompanied by Rustem's mandolin. Zina asked Rustem to show her how to play it, though more out of amusement than any serious attempt to learn:

she enjoyed being the centre of attention. The discussions once again returned to the topic of love, although it is not known who raised the subject. Towards the end of the evening, a suggestion was made by someone that they should start a separate notebook for ideas anyone might have on their expedition. Eventually they all made their way inside the tent to prepare to sleep for the night and this was when a terrible argument broke out. No one wanted to sleep by the stove, which was just inside the entrance at the front of the tent. It appears that a group decision was made (the diary states 'we agree that Yurka Kri will sleep there') that George Krivonischenko be nominated to sleep there, without any recourse or discussion with him. Possibly Igor Dyatlov as group leader told him that he was nominated to spend the night there. However, the decision was reached and the result was an explosion of temper from Krivonischenko, who started swearing and accusing the others that they had 'betrayed him'. This must have brought a rejoinder from at least some of the others, because although he moved to take his position next to the stove, the furious Krivonischenko continued shouting and arguing for some time after they had bedded down and they were unable to get to sleep for some time due to the commotion. Whilst the outburst of temper from Krivonischenko may have taken them all by surprise, he possibly had some justification as he had already slept on the floor of the hotel in Vizhay only three days previously in order to allow the others to sleep in the beds. Whether or not his anger was justified, the incident showed that Krivonischenko had a very short fuse.

The effect of the furious row must have spilled over into the following day (29 January). There is a short, terse two-line diary entry by Nicolai Thibeaux-Brignolle describing the route they take, which ends with 'That is it'. Yet no mention is made of the argument in the tent the previous night. This second day of their journey into the mountains saw them move from the River Lozva to the River Auspia, a right-hand tributary. The group travelled along a sleigh-and-deer trail on the riverbank used by Mansi hunters. With a weak wind and the temperature at -13°C, the only thing mentioned in the diary for that day is the occasional appearance of ice in the River Lozva.

They tried to make good progress on 30 January as the weather was noticeably colder and they wanted to move north from the route they were following along the River Auspia. They had spent the third night camped on the shore of the river and with the approach of night the temperature had plunged to -26°C. The morning temperatures were between -13°C and -17°C. The temperature and conditions were described as typical for the Urals.

The home-made stove constructed by Igor Dyatlov was said to be doing 'a great job'. George Krivonischenko made the suggestion that they should make steam heat in the tent; the cold was obviously affecting them. It is not known who made the diary entry for 30 January but an entry stated that the curtains hung inside the tent 'were quite justified': it is not known if this is a reference to privacy or whether the curtains acted as further insulation from the cold by compartmentalising the tent's interior.

They rose at 8.30 a.m. on 30 January, had breakfast and then departed. The group diary was written while on the go. Their progress along the Auspia River was impeded by ice dams although there was not enough ice to actually walk on the river itself, so they moved slightly inland to a sledge trail used by the Mansi. This third day on foot and skis saw them moving into the territory used by the Mansi, and reference was made to the tribe and their use of signs and markings on the trees they passed, which signi-fied how many local hunters had passed along the trail and to which family clan they belonged. Some of the markings also referred to the types of animals in the area. The sledge and deer trail gradually petered out and the forest itself also started thinning out as the trees became shorter, with mention of dwarf birches and pines. As they started moving out of the thicker forest, they looked for a suitable place to camp and eventually settled on a spot near some trees. There was a strong west wind that was blowing snow off the cedar and pine trees, giving the effect of falling snow. The tent was erected on a bed of spruce branches and they built a fire to warm themselves before sleep.

On 31 January the sky was clear but there was a strong west wind that was causing snow to fall from the tops of the trees. The temperature was between -18°C and -24°C. It is recorded that they gradually left the Auspia Valley making slow progress (roughly 1 mile per hour). They took an old beaten Mansi trail that they noticed had been used fairly recently by a Mansi hunter. The ground was starting to rise gradually and the going was hard with low visibility. The group was forced to find a new method of clearing a path for the skis: walking in single file, the first one dropped his/her rucksack and walked forward, making the trail in the deep snow for a period of approximately five minutes. He/she could move quicker than the rest of the group. The group continued following the person up front without the rucksack. Movement was always difficult for the second person in the file because the snow had not properly compacted and they would be carrying a full load. After five minutes of clearing the way, the first one went back to their rucksack, took a short rest and then caught up with the group. This person then became the last in the file but the going was easier for them because the snow was now compacted by the eight people in front. The file would continue with each taking their turn. As they left the Auspia valley, the ground continued to rise but was smooth. They prepared to pitch their tent at around 4 p.m. to 5 p.m. that afternoon. The snow cover was 1.22m (4ft) thick and was still falling.

They spent the night of 31 January at the very edge of the forest before continuing the following day (Sunday 1 February). The final part of the last entry in the diary states:

> Tired and exhausted, we start to prepare the platform for the tent. Firewood is not enough. We didn't dig a hole for a fire. Too tired for that. We had supper right in the tent. Hard to imagine such a comfort somewhere on the ridge, with a piercing wind, hundreds (of) kilometres away from human settlements.

Nothing is known of the remainder of their journey to the mountain pass on Kholat Syakhl as no diary entry was made for this day (1 February). The group would have risen as normal, packed up the tent and their gear, and once again made their slow way onwards to their destination. At some point on the afternoon of 1 February they decided to pitch their tent on the pass at Kholat Syakhl, where it was eventually found by the search party. The sun set at 5.02 p.m. on that day so it would have been some time before that when they set up camp. An unusual aspect of the site they chose is that they appear to have lost their way and ended up on the eastern slope of Kholat Syakhl ('Mountain of the Dead') rather than on Mount Otorten ('don't go there') as they had originally intended. There are no entries in the diary to say why this is and, in fact, the last entry in the diary on the previous day merely concerns itself with practicalities, with a final comment about a piercing wind and the fact that they are miles away from civilisation. There is no reference or seeming awareness that they are in the wrong place and not in their intended destination.

Considering they were all well experienced in hiking and ski tourism, which entailed map reading, it appears an odd error to make. Mount Otorten lay 9 miles (15km) directly to the north of where they were. One of the last photographs taken of the group on their final day (1 February) shows them in a line moving forward but the visibility is very poor. However, it is possible that as they made their way up from the tree line, they could have been aware of where they were, but with darkness falling decided to pitch their tent and correct their bearings the following morning. Another of the final photographs shows what appears to be Zina Kolmogorova wrapping a bandage around the ankle of Alexander Kolevatov while the others in the group dig out the snow to prepare the area for pitching their tent.

On this last stop, they were obviously ready for sleep, having reached the point of exhaustion after travelling for the whole day. This final stage of their journey was tough for them as the ground was getting steeper. In the days leading up to this, the tone is noticeably subdued and the high spirits and exuberance apparent in the earlier photos and diary entries had disappeared. From the final diary entry onwards, everything is conjecture, up to the bodies being discovered by the search parties.

On the last evening, after the tent had been pitched, the party were preparing to eat their supper and would have been getting ready to bed down for the night. At some stage after this, something happened that caused them to panic and exit the tent as fast as possible. Whatever it was, it created such alarm that in their panic they slashed their way out of the tent using knives so as to get away as quickly as possible rather than open the tent at the front. In their rush, they left behind knives, hatchets, shoes (each had two pairs – one for outside and one soft pair for inside the tent) as well as warm clothes. In other words, they left behind everything that would enable them to survive the harsh winter conditions they faced outside the tent. When the tent was later examined, it could be seen that two large gashes had been made to allow someone of adult size to get through. The bottom part of the gashes had been cut right across the tent, in effect almost removing the whole side of the tent. There had also been smaller slit holes made at crouching height, which looked as if they may have made these first in order to look outside the tent to see what was there. Assuming they had used knives to damage the tent so they could see what was outside, rather than going out through the front, shows that whatever was outside the tent was deeply alarming and probably life threatening.

Nothing is known about what caused the group to behave in such a completely irrational way, which would lead to their certain deaths once they had left the confines of the tent.

2

USSR and the world in 1959

Despite the events of the night of 1/2 February being more than fifty years ago at the time of writing, it is still well within the living memory of many people. The geopolitical situation has completely changed in that time and these changes have probably been more marked in the present-day Russian Federation than anywhere else.

In January 1959, a number of the Dyatlov group were students at Ural Polytechnic Institute (UPI) and their day-to-day lives were dominated by the background of the Cold War, particularly as the city they were living and studying in (Sverdlovsk) was the centre of a large region containing nuclear, industrial and military facilities that were all geared towards achieving dominance over capitalism in the USA and the West. Control of the numerous military facilities for the whole region came under the Ural Military District, which had sent over 2 million men to fight against the Nazis during the Second World War. As will be examined in later chapters, a number of the military aspects of the Cold War are to surface in more than one theory concerning the fate of the Dyatlov group.

Despite the death of Josef Stalin six years previously, the Soviet Union in 1959 was still a repressive state ruled with an iron rod by the Communist Party under the premier, Nikita Khrushchev, who had come through the war years as a political commissar and was a shrewd politician. Khrushchev ensured the removal of his main rival for power, Lavrenti Beria, the Minister of the Interior under Stalin.

The tragedy that befell the Dyatlov group is best understood in terms of the Cold War: in some of the theories as to what actually happened to them, and also in understanding their behaviour as good young communists.

The Cold War can be loosely described as the United States of America and the Soviet Union eyeing each other warily like two prizefighters pacing around a ring waiting for the fight to begin, with their supporters (NATO and the Warsaw Pact) in each corner waiting to jump into the ring and join in the fight as soon as it started.

After the end of the Korean War, the Cold War tension started to build up again in 1956 with a perception by the USA of what was known as the 'Bomber Gap'. This was a term used to describe what the USA felt was a superiority in numbers of long-range bombers by the Soviet Air Force over the US Air Force. It was a completely erroneous view and had arisen as a result of growing concerns of Soviet bomber numbers and capabilities after the first mention in the West in February 1954 of the new Myasishchev M-4 (NATO codenamed Bison) bomber. The issue was exacerbated as a result of an observation at the Aviation Day at Tushino Airfield in Moscow in July 1955 when ten M-4 Bison bombers flew past the viewing stands and then, unknown to the majority of the observers on the ground, flew around and repeated the flypast no fewer than six times, which led the observers to think that a total of 60 M-4 Bisons had taken part in the flypast.[1] Analysts in the West worked out that at this rate of production, the USSR would build 600 bombers in a very short period of time. President Eisenhower did not believe the numbers, and the deployment of U-2 spy flights over the USSR was to eventually prove this to be the case, but that had not stopped massive resources being poured into the US Air Force to build up a gigantic fleet of its own bombers (over 2,000 Boeing B-47s and well over 700 Boeing B-52s).

The 'Bomber Gap' was followed by the 'Missile Gap'. In 1957 the term 'Missile Gap' was used to describe the disparity between the numbers and power of Intercontinental Ballistic Missiles (ICBMs) between the USA and the USSR, with the numbers held by the Russians considered to be vastly superior in quantity and power to the US arsenal. The estimates that had been put forward in a report by the Security Resources Panel of the President's Science Advisory Committee (known as the Gaither Committee) were totally incorrect, but had basically been a useful way of frightening an already jittery voting public into going along with vast increases in military budgets in order to close the so-called 'gap'. The 'Missile Gap' disappeared with the production of a CIA National Intelligence Estimate on 3 November 1959.

These events were compounded by the launch of the world's first space satellite, *Sputnik 1*, on 4 October 1957, which gave the impression that the Soviet Union was leading the Americans in what became known as the Space Race.

The Cold War had not quite reached its height and the Cuban Missile Crisis was still over three and a half years away when, in the same month that the Dyatlov group set out on their fateful journey, Che Guevara and Camilo Cienfuegos entered Havana in Cuba – on 4 January 1959 – with Fidel Castro entering the city two days later. The following day, 7 January 1959, the USA recognised Fidel Castro's new government. Fulgencio Batista had officially been ousted and Castro became Prime Minister on 16 February 1959.

The reality of the Cold War was to come close to Sverdlovsk when Francis Gary Powers was shot down by an S-75 missile (NATO codename SA-2 Guideline) on 1 May 1960 in his Lockheed U2 spy plane near to the village of Kosulino, not far from where the Dyatlov group had set off on their fateful journey just over a year earlier in January 1959. Powers was first detained by residents of Kosulino, who initially thought he was a Soviet cosmonaut who had returned to earth.

Over in the USA in 1959 Alaska had just become the forty-ninth US state, and the contrast between the day-to-day life in the USA with the dour austere life in the USSR could not have been greater. Despite colossal spending on the military, Khrushchev had wanted to improve the lot of the average Soviet citizen and looked to improve the quality of life in a number of areas. While Khrushchev pondered the question of raising Soviet living standards, the American Dream was being played out in full in the USA. Whereas students and young people in the USSR, like the Dyatlov group, tried to find their entertainment in activities such as hiking to remote areas where conversation and ideas could be freely expressed, their counterparts in the USA were immersed in pop culture: R. Berry Gordy Jr founded Motown Records on 12 January 1959; 3 February 1959 was the 'day the music died' when Buddy Holly, Ritchie Valens and J.P. Richardson (the Big Bopper) were in a Beechcraft Bonanza piloted by Roger Peterson when it crashed near Clear Lake, Iowa, killing all four of them; the Marx Brothers made their last TV appearance in *The Incredible Jewel Robbery* on 8 March 1959; the following day, the Barbie doll made its debut at the American International Toy Fair in New York (9 March 1959 is also Barbie's official birth date incidentally).

Against the backdrop of the American Dream, the arms race and space race were taken as seriously by the Americans as by the Russians. The Americans were pushing ahead with their quest for dominance in ICBMs, with the first successful firing of a Titan ICBM at Cape Canaveral on 6 February 1959. This was later followed by the launch of the submarine USS *George Washington* on 9 June 1959, becoming the first sub to carry ballistic missiles. On 9 April 1959 NASA announced its selection of seven military pilots for astronaut training – to become the first US astronauts. On 28 May 1959 the Americans sent into space a pair of monkeys named Able and Miss Baker, aboard a Jupiter AM-18 rocket, as the first living beings to successfully return to Earth from space.

On 2 January 1959 the USSR launched *Luna 1* from Baikonur, which was the first spacecraft to travel to the vicinity of the Moon. The Americans kept up with the launch of their *Pioneer 4* mission two months later on 3 March 1959. What the Russians could not keep up with in nuclear and space developments, they had an army of spies to get the information for them. On 23 June 1959, Klaus Fuchs, the atomic spy who had worked on the Manhattan Project and was arrested in Britain for passing nuclear secrets to the Russians, was released from his fourteen-year jail term after nine years and allowed to return behind the Iron Curtain to Dresden in East Germany, where he resumed his scientific career.

This intense rivalry between the USSR and the USA extended to all areas, not just military. It was also not just rivalry between the governments of two superpowers, but rivalry between two completely opposing systems: communism versus capitalism. Everything from sport to technology was touted as being superior to the other. This fierce rivalry is best illustrated in one example that took place on 24 July 1959.

Known as the 'Kitchen Debate', Vice-President Richard Nixon was visiting Moscow and was at the opening of the American National Exhibition in Sokolniki Park. Also present at the opening was Nikita Khrushchev. An entire house was built for the exhibition and presented as the type of house that anyone in America could afford.[2] The house had been cut in half to make viewing easier and Khrushchev and Nixon had engaged in discussions through their respective interpreters as to the respective merits of their systems of government and accomplishments. The discussions took place in a number of locations at the exhibition but primarily in the kitchen of the American showhouse. Khrushchev pushed his view that the Soviets concentrated on things that mattered and not on luxury. He sarcastically asked of Nixon if they (the Americans) 'had a washing machine that puts food in the mouth and pushes it down'. Nixon's response was that at least their argument was more to do with technology than military.[3] Both men eventually agreed that their two countries should be more open with each other. Khrushchev was sceptical that his remarks would not be translated and broadcast as he intended – to state the Communist case for wanting peace and improving the lot of the ordinary man – in the USA, but they were, and in colour videotape, which was new at the time. Nixon's remarks were only partially translated into Russian and the debate broadcast late at night in the USSR. Up to this point, Nixon had had a fairly ambivalent relationship with the American public. However, despite mixed reviews in the American press, Nixon's standing was enhanced as a result of the debate, as many felt he had stood up firmly to Khrushchev's blustering bully persona.

In the rest of the world, notably the other Communist giant, China, Liu Shaoqi succeeded Mao Tse Tung as Chairman of the People's Republic on 27 April 1959. In Britain, Harold Macmillan was letting go of overseas possessions and Cyprus was granted independence on 19 February 1959. Not long afterwards, on 3 June 1959, Singapore became a self-governing colony with Lee Kwan Yew as premier.

In France, Charles de Gaulle was inaugurated as the fifth president of the French Fifth Republic on 8 January 1959 and slowly set about taking France out of NATO. In Switzerland, on 1 February 1959 a referendum turned down female suffrage. Against this setback for women in Switzerland, in Nepal women voted for the first time less than three weeks later on 18 February 1959.

Ski tourism
in the USSR

Life was grey and austere in the 1950s Soviet Union. The same could also have been said of Britain and many other countries in the West, although things were starting to change in Britain and teenagers at least had outlets and interests such as rock and roll (and Teddy Boys could kick the hell out of each other to their hearts' content). Life for students in 1959 Sverdlovsk was very different and there were few outlets for their energies in their spare time. One outlet, of course, was sport, but this was still rigorously controlled by the state.

The whole concept of 'sport' occupied a different place in Soviet society to that in the West. It came under the control of the powerful All-Union Committee on Physical Culture and Sports Affairs until its dissolution in 1959, the year of the Dyatlov tragedy (although its dissolution was nothing to do with the tragedy itself). The official Soviet view was that sport was part of physical culture, which had four components: organised physical education, playful activities or games, all forms of (socially approved) active leisure pursuits and organised sports. Active leisure pursuits were included in physical culture as long as they were considered to add to the physical and mental well-being of the individual or the community in general. The other aspect of sport from an official point of view was that there was a constant emphasis to prepare the younger generation not just for a healthy future life but also to be better workers and to better enable them in support of the defence of their socialist homeland. Sport was officially viewed as combating anti-social behaviour in town and countryside. Lenin himself had been a keen sportsman and viewed it as a vital activity. His views were close to that of the English 'muscular Christians' such as Dr Thomas Arnold, the headmaster of Rugby School, and the novelists Thomas Hughes and Charles Kingsley, who all promoted the concept of 'a healthy mind in a healthy body'.[1]

After the Second World War, sport in Russia was seen by the government as a means of continuing peacefully the war against the remaining enemy – the bourgeois-democratic states of the world. Physical education was compulsory at Soviet colleges and universities for all students in the first two years. Within the Ural Polytechnic Institute (in common with similar Soviet establishments) great emphasis was placed on sports, and virtually every year from 1956 onwards, the 'Student Spring' was held by the students, with many competitions being staged. The 'Student Spring' became known as 'UPI Spring' but was not held in 1959, partly as a reaction to the Dyatlov tragedy and also because the authorities did not want any demonstrations. All the members of the Dyatlov group were keen on these sports events and particularly 'UPI Spring'. 'UPI Spring' itself was moved as a yearly event from the confines of the university to the Lenin Prospekt main street, which runs from the park area in front of the main entrance to the university through the centre of Ekaterinburg (Sverdlovsk).

Although 'UPI Spring' is still held at the same time every year, it has changed from being a one-day intensive sporting event to a series of sports events and cultural seminars held over a period of three to four weeks, and includes international participation. The scene looking down from the front of the university towards Lenin Prospekt is essentially unchanged from 1959, apart from some of the newer, taller buildings.

For a student in 1959 Sverdlovsk, the opportunity for having 'a good time' had narrower possibilities than for a student in the West. Anything that attracted more than a frown from the mirthless views of the Soviet state could end up with a charge of 'hooliganism'. After university registration, all new students were sent to work on a *kolkhoz* (collective farm) for two weeks, which was intended for the students to get to know each other and foster solidarity between themselves and the farm workers.

One activity that was popular among students was 'tourism'. This was a wide term that covered organised outdoor activities and included hiking, camping, rock climbing and skiing. Ski tourism, which came under this general description, was very popular among students. It meant a group of friends or like-minded individuals could have the chance to get away from the day-to-day grind of their lives and enjoy themselves while participating in an officially sanctioned activity, as it involved group participation that promoted solidarity. It should not be viewed that this was an excuse for a bunch of guys and gals to grab a stash of booze and head into the mountains for a two-week orgy. What the Dyatlov group were attempting to do demanded the highest levels of fitness and orienteering skills, but one main reason it was popular is that it gave them the chance to let their hair down and relax without being watched or listened to constantly.

The description 'ski tourism' has modern-day connotations of an organised package holiday group in which a group of skiers pay their money and have everything laid on for them to enjoy a skiing holiday at the resort of their choice. In the late 1950s in the USSR, the description had a very different meaning in that it referred to a more organised activity with rules and control by the university (in the Dyatlov case) and state control. It was also considered to be a sport that demanded high levels of physical fitness and orienteering skills, which could be adapted to military requirements.

The trip organised by the Dyatlov group was dedicated in honour of the 21st Communist Party Congress being held in Moscow between 27 January and 5 February 1959. It may appear odd that a provincial sports party in the middle of the country should dedicate their forthcoming trip to a political meeting being held by the ruling political party. It would be similar, say, to a group of mountaineering students at Edinburgh University dedicating their next mountain climb to a forthcoming Labour Party Convention being held in Blackpool, or the Miami Hurricanes American Football team at Miami University dedicating their hardest won game of the season to the Republican Party National Convention in Tampa. However, the Communist Party was central to daily life in the USSR and no observance of that fact could be too great or considered over the top in whatever form it was expressed. It is also worth noting that when Stalin was in power, Soviet mountaineers would often carry a bust of Stalin to the top of the highest peaks. The highest Soviet peak, a 24,590ft (7,495m) mountain in the Pamir Range, was named Stalin Peak during his premiership and in 1962 was renamed Communism Peak. With the break-up of the USSR, the mountain now lies in Tajikistan and was renamed Ismoil Somoni Peak in 1998.

It would be hard to imagine any American mountaineer carrying a bust of the serving US President to the top of Mount McKinley. Similarly, a British climber carrying a bust of the current British Prime Minister to the top of Snowden or Ben Nevis in adulation would probably be thought of as strange.

Yet this was the situation in the Soviet Union at the time and anybody who did not wish to play by the rules found that life would rapidly start getting very difficult for them.

4

The Dyatlov group and Mount Otorten

Although the group are all usually described as students of UPI (Ural Polytechnic Institute), in reality only six of them were students at the time of the tragedy – Igor Dyatlov, the two young women Zina Kolmogorova and Luda Dubinina, Alexander Kolevatov, Yury Yudin and Yury Doroshenko.

Igor Dyatlov, born 13 January 1936, was the group leader and had considerable experience of ski tourism, to the extent that he was considered a professional ski tourist, having been the leader of numerous tourist groups on hikes of different categories of complexity. Dyatlov had already been asked to stay on after his graduation (due to take place later in 1959) and continue to work at the university in his capacity as an experienced ski tourist. He had also made three previous ski tourism trips to the northern Urals. He was considered to be a modest, honest and considerate man who did not rush his decisions. It was said that he was very hard on people on the ski trips but he felt that discipline needed to be imposed on these trips for safety reasons; he would not tolerate a 'shirker'. At the time of the tragedy he was a fifth-year student in the Faculty of Radio Engineering. During his second year he had designed and built a radio that he had used on hikes in the Ural Mountains in 1956. He had also designed an extremely functional small stove, which he had taken with him on

44

trips in 1958 and also on the final and fateful trip in 1959. As well as his engineering skills, he liked to play the mandolin. He was very fond of Zina Kolmogorova and she appeared to reciprocate his feelings, despite the fact she had previously been in a relationship with Yury Doroshenko, who was also in the group. A photograph of Zina was found on Igor Dyatlov's body by the search parties. As leader of the group Igor was responsible for planning the route of their journey to Mount Otorten from Sverdlovsk.

Semyon Zolotarev, born 2 February 1921, introduced himself to the others as Alexander.[1] He was the oldest member of the group at 37 years old, the rest being between 20 and 25 years old, although all of them were experienced ski tourists. Semyon's death was very early in the morning of his 38th birthday. His involvement with the Dyatlov group tends to attract the most attention from researchers as he was much older than the rest and had what could be described as a more 'mysterious' background and character. His background was also very different to the others. He was born in Kuban in the North Caucasus to Cossack parents (his father Aleksay Zolotarev was a paramedic). From October 1941 to May 1946 Semyon was in the military (attaining the rank of sergeant in the Russian Army) and served in the Second World War (or, more correctly, the Great Patriotic War). He joined the Communist Party after the war and, just prior to leaving the military, he transferred to the Leningrad Military Engineering University in April 1946. After this, he appeared to drift somewhat, transferring first to the Minsk Institute of Physical Education (known by its acronym GIFKB) and later he became a tourist guide in Artybash, Altai in southern Siberia. People who knew Zolotarev when he worked as a tourist guide in Altai described him as not being very good at his work and that he appeared to be more interested in drinking and womanising. Adding to his mystery was a number of tattoos that he generally took care to keep hidden. While it is possible he may have been embarrassed by them, tattoos then, as now, have particular meaning in Russia as they are used to signify status within the Russian criminal underworld. Few criminals would dare to wear tattoos they had not earned. There is, however, controversy over Zolotarev's tattoos, which can be seen in a picture of his body at the autopsy. His sister said that he had never had any tattoos.

However, the 'mysterious' background, which tends more to focus on his involvement in the war with Germany, is not quite so mysterious when one considers that he was 20 years old when Germany attacked the USSR in June 1941 and was therefore of prime military call-up age. Unlike other members of the group, there are no living witnesses who remember him well, and what is known of his time in Sverdlovsk and at UPI is very little. Yury Yudin remembers him from that time and says that he had great respect for him and that some of the talk of Zolotarev having been in prison or a fugitive convict was nonsense. At the time of his joining the group for the trip to Mount Otorten, Zolotarev was an instructor at the Kourovskaya tourist base.

Alexander Kolevatov, born 16 November 1934, by the time he had entered UPI as a physics student had already studied metallurgy of heavy non-ferrous metals at the Sverdlovsk Mining and Metallurgy College. He was an exceptional student and transferred to Moscow to work in a secret laboratory (known as Laboratory B), which was organised within Department 9 of the NKVD (the secret police and forerunner of the KGB). The laboratory was relocated to Chelyabinsk and its main goal was developing protection from ionising radiation. The laboratory gradually grew into an institute that was known simply as 3394 (its PO Box No – 3394). It was later subordinated to the Ministry of Medium

Machine Building. From here, Kolevatov transferred to the Research Institute of Inorganic Materials, where he was involved in the production of materials for nuclear use. In 1956 he returned to Sverdlovsk to study physics at Ural Polytechnic Institute. At the time of the tragedy he was a fourth-year student in the Faculty of Technical Physics and was described as diligent, methodical and pedantic, with leadership qualities. A studio photograph of him shows an assured and intense-looking young man. His manner and meticulous attention to detail led the two girls in the group to dislike him and describe him as 'a regular bore'. Despite his pedantic qualities, which included an opinion on every subject, he did have a sense of humour and could be a comic when he wanted to be. He composed humorous verse and Yury Yudin possessed one of these verses he had received from Kolevatov on a New Year card. Along with some of the other males in the group he could also play the mandolin, but not very well.

George Krivonischenko, born 7 February 1935, had graduated from UPI and was a qualified engineer. He had worked as an engineer at Chelyabinsk-40, the secret, closed nuclear city south of Sverdlovsk, and was part of a group involved in the clean-up after what was known as the Kyshtym nuclear accident in September 1957. Kyshtym is a small city 6 miles (10km) from Chelyabinsk-40 where the accident happened. Some commentators have suggested that the radioactivity measured on the clothes of some of the group after they were found dead might have been related to this accident, but it is most unlikely that Krivonischenko would still be wearing the same clothes, as the accident had occurred two years previously. Krivonischenko was very much looking forward to the trip and had written in a letter to friends in December 1958: 'Frankly speaking, I am longing for camp life and think of a trip as of a great blessing.'

Rustem Slobodin, born 11 January 1936, was an ethnic Russian but, in keeping with communist ideals, had been given a Tartar first name by his parents in recognition of friendship and solidarity with other ethnic groups. Like George Krivonischenko, he had also graduated from UPI in 1959 and was an engineer. Those who knew him described him as quiet and thoughtful, as well as honest and decent. Yury Yudin described Rustem as a real 'diamond', very likeable and amiable. In addition to a very high level of fitness, which he maintained by running in all weathers, he also enjoyed trekking and hiking, and would take his mandolin on these trips. His father was a professor at another Sverdlovsk higher educational establishment.

Yury Doroshenko, born 12 January 1938, had been involved in a relationship with Zina Kolmogorova, which was serious enough for them to have visited her parents in Kamensk-Urals. He was a student at UPI but the relationship with Zina had finished and she had become friendly with Igor Dyatlov by the time of their journey to Kholat Syakhl. Despite the break-up of their relationship and her apparent feelings towards Igor Dyatlov, Yury remained on good terms with both of them. He was modest and reserved and generally tried not to show his emotions.

Lyudmila 'Luda' Dubinina, born 12 May 1938, came from a family of intellectuals and was a third-year student at UPI studying engineering and economics. A gregarious young woman, she was active in the Tourist Club and enjoyed singing and photography. She was also an experienced ski tourist, having led a group to the northern Urals the previous winter of 1958. Many of the photos on the trip to Kholat Syakhl were taken by her. On one Tourist Club trip to the Eastern Sayan Mountains two years prior to their final journey to Kholat Syakhl, she had been accidentally shot by another member of the group who was cleaning his rifle. Despite being non-life-threatening, it was a painful wound which she bore with good humour on the journey to receive medical attention. She was also a very forthright and outspoken girl who held strong opinions. Her enthusiasm could be summed up in the phrase she used from time to time, 'For the Motherland! For Stalin!'[2] It was said of her that she would not hesitate to tell someone straight to their face if she thought they were wrong in any way. One comment has been made of her, that when her body was found after the tragedy, the fact that her tongue was missing may have been due to her forthrightness and outspokenness, depending on which theory is referred to.

Zinaida 'Zina' Kolmogorova, born 12 January 1937, was a very attractive young woman in her fourth year at UPI, studying radio engineering. Zina was outgoing and attracted people to her because of her good-natured disposition. It was said of her that she filled a room with her personality. Although she often described herself as just a 'country girl', she was highly intelligent and a good organiser. Zina was considered to be the life and soul of the Tourist Club at the university. She was also an experienced hiker and, like Luda Dubinina, she had also suffered a misfortune on one trip when she was bitten by a viper. She had refused help in carrying her load before getting medical help. Again like Luda Dubinina, she displayed heroic qualities, which would be expected of good young communists who would bear any suffering or burden with stoicism. She was outgoing, confident and fully aware of her looks. A comment was made about her that with her personality and intelligence, had she lived, she had the potential to become a Minister of the USSR.

Zina was in a relationship (or at least emotionally involved) with the group leader Igor Dyatlov. However, she did not join the group just because of her attachment to him. Rather it was because this trip was expected to be shorter than another trip being undertaken by members of the university at the same time that she had originally considered joining. She had previously been involved in a relationship with another member of the Dyatlov group, Yury Doroshenko, and there was also a third member of the Dyatlov group who appeared to have designs on her, Semyon Zolotarev. She was therefore the subject of attention from three of the seven males in the group (leaving out Yury Yudin who left the group before they went into the mountains) and this potentially volatile mix of young men vying for her attention is the focus of one of the theories of what happened on the night of 1/2 February 1959.

Nicolai Thibeaux-Brignolle ('Tibo'), born 5 June 1935, as his name suggests was very different to the rest of the group. He was the son of a French communist who had been executed during the period when Stalin was in power. Nicolai had, in fact, been born in a prison camp for political prisoners. His father had made a significant contribution to the industrial development of the Urals region but had fallen out of favour with those in power. Despite these apparent handicaps and the 'thaw' after Khrushchev took over the USSR, Nicolai had attended UPI and graduated (in civil engineering) the previous year before the trip to Kholat Syakhl. He was popular and had a friendly character, a good sense of humour and liked to play practical jokes. He also appeared to have had access to a great deal of literature that was not available to others in those times.

Yury Yudin, born 19 July 1937, was the only survivor of the ten that set out on the fateful journey from Sverdlovsk on 23 January 1959. A fourth-year student in the Faculty of Engineering and Economics at UPI, he was also an experienced hiker. Like both the females in the group, he too had experienced an injury (an injured back) on a previous hiking expedition and it was recurring pain from this injury that saved his life when he decided to abandon the trip and return to Sverdlovsk. Yury Yudin was an economist; he is sometimes incorrectly described as a geologist, probably due to his search for minerals at the second severny just prior to leaving the group to return to Sverdlovsk on 28 January 1959. In October 2012 he was asked to describe himself at a meeting in Ekaterinburg, to which he replied by saying he considered himself to be a 'regular booby'. Igor Dyatlov had asked him twice to go on the trip and he accepted the second time, as he said he liked to be around Igor Dyatlov, who was always brimming with interesting ideas. Despite Yudin's self-deprecation, Igor Dyatlov obviously valued Yudin's organisational skills and asked him to look after the medical side of things as well as the equipment and food supplies. Yury had been asked by the Minerals Museum at the university to bring back samples for them.

As mentioned in Chapter 1, there was also an eleventh member of the group named Nicolai Popov, who was good friends with the others and had fully intended to travel to Mount Otorten with them on 23 January. However, he missed the train at Sverdlovsk railway station and stayed behind: something he was no doubt very grateful for. Popov was still alive in 2012 and lived in Ekaterinburg.

Sogrin group

At the time of the planned Dyatlov group journey, there was another group planning an expedition into the northern Urals, the Sogrin group, which both Semyon Zolotarev and Zina Kolmogorova had intended to join. However, this group were planning a different route that was going to take some considerable time longer than the Dyatlov-planned journey. For this reason, Semyon Zolotarev and

Zina Kolmogorova both changed their minds and joined the Dyatlov expedition instead. Zolotarev was planning on heading home to his family after the planned expedition and did not want to be away as long as the Sogrin group were planning. Zina Kolmogorova also wanted a shorter time away and there is a suggestion that she was the first to change her mind and switch to the Dyatlov group. The suggestion goes on to say that she was then followed by Semyon Zolotarev, who found her very attractive (despite his being considerably older), so that he could be close to her.

Mount Otorten and the Mansi

The aim of the group was to trek initially to the 4,048ft (1,234m) Mount Otorten in the northern Ural Mountains 340 miles (550km) north of Sverdlovsk. The original planned route to Mount Otorten was to be Sverdlovsk – Serov – Ivdel – Vizhay – the second severny (an abandoned settlement) – Mount Otorten. Beyond Mount Otorten, the group intended to go on to Mount Oika-Chakur and the River North Toshemka before returning the same way via Vizhay, Ivdel, Serov and finally Sverdlovsk. The trek was to be a good test of the group's capabilities, as it was in a very remote location and would take place in midwinter when weather conditions would be at their harshest. The rating/ranking for the trip was level 3 – the highest level of complexity. ('Complexity' is the most direct translation, but a better word for English ears would be 'difficulty', as in the rating of a chess problem.)

As already mentioned, Mount Otorten in the local Mansi language translates as 'don't go there'. Rather than any ominous warning to would-be travellers, it was more intended to signify a place that was difficult to reach in winter and was best avoided in difficult conditions. Mount Otorten stood on the border of the Sverdlovsk Oblast and the KOMI autonomous republic, close to the border of the Perm and Tyumen Oblasts. This was the northernmost point of the Sverdlovsk Oblast and the source of the River Lozva is located in the vicinity of this mountain. The area surrounding Mount Otorten was very sparsely populated, primarily by the Mansi tribe, hunters who had lived in the region for hundreds of years. The first mention of them in written records was in 1396[3] when they were described in Russian chronicles as Voguls. The term Vogul came from the Komi and Khant languages of the respective tribes who lived in nearby regions. The Mansi were to be known as Voguls for many years until the term Mansi was first used by Russians in 1785.[4] The term Mansi (*Maan's'i* literally means human or man in their language) became common usage from the 1920s onwards within the Soviet Union. The Mansi folklore and traditions are rich with legends connected to their way of life and the land in which they live.[5]

The area the Mansi occupy (the Khanty-Mansi National District) in north-west Siberia is huge, covering 523,100km/sq in the Tyumen region. They have always tended to live in the river valleys such as the villages of Konda, Lozva, Pelym and Tavda, which stretch from the Ural Mountains to the lower reaches of the River Ob. Despite the vast area of their territory, the Mansi have always been small in numbers. A census in 1897 put their total population at 7,600.[6] A census carried out in 1959, the year of the Dyatlov tragedy, put their total population at 6,449 with 59.2 per cent of them being native speakers of the Mansi language.[7]

One well-known member of the Mansi is Mayor Sergey Semenovich Sobyanin, the Mayor of Moscow City (from 21 October 2012).

5

Aftermath
and autopsies

The search

The Dyatlov group had been due to arrive back in
Sverdlovsk on 14–15 February 1959, and the return of Yury
Yudin to Sverdlovsk on 28 January 1959 must have given
the impression that things were proceeding as normal.
Yudin had retraced his steps and returned to Sverdlovsk via
Vizhay and Ivdel. As it was still university vacation time,
he went to stay with his parents in the Taborinsky district
of Sverdlovsk.

The group did not have a radio and the first indication
that all was not well was on 12 February when Igor Dyatlov
was meant to send a message by telegram to the university
from Vizhay, confirming that the trip was virtually complete and they were in Vizhay on their way back. When
the telegram did not arrive, there was no undue alarm, as
given the nature of the trip allowances had to be made for
the weather affecting the pace of travel. The Yury Blinov
group with whom they had left Sverdlovsk and travelled
north had returned to Sverdlovsk and reported that there
had been a heavy snowstorm in the area of Kholat Syakhl,
although at this point it would not have been known that
that is where the Dyatlov group was, although it was close
to Mount Otorten. This information led officials to believe
that in the case of bad weather the group would err on the

side of caution and try to take shelter until the weather improved enough for them to resume their journey.

As time passed with no sign of them, nor the receipt of any message, friends, relatives and parents started to get worried. People who knew Igor Dyatlov were particularly worried, as they knew that as group leader he took particular care over procedures and would have been concerned that a message had not been sent. Whilst the worst may not have been feared at this stage, an ominous sense of foreboding grew. Worried parents made calls to the UPI Sports Club and the City Sports Club in Sverdlovsk (later Ekaterinburg), as did other ski tourists who knew Igor Dyatlov, calling for a search party to be organised.

Nonetheless, despite the apparent lack of concern over the delay in the return of the group, the relatives of both Luda Dubinina and Alexander Kolevatov pressed the head of the University Sports Club, Lev Gordo, strongly enough for him to make an unfortunate and untruthful statement to them. On the wrong assumption that the group had been delayed by the weather and they would shortly appear, he told them that he was in receipt of a telegram from Igor Dyatlov informing them of the delay in the group's return. While he presumably felt he had done this with the best of intentions in order to allay their fears, it only led to a further delay in a search being organised. There was also some confusion, as Yury Blinov's group who had travelled north with the Dyatlov group had actually sent a telegram back to the university at this time to say that they were on their way back.

More time passed and, with no further news, relatives of the group complained to senior members of the local Communist Party. The Dyatlov group trip had been organised in honour of the 21st Communist Party Congress held in Moscow from 27 January to 5 February 1959 and something had to be done as the negative publicity would not have looked good, even despite the level of censorship in the USSR. Finally, on 20 February it was agreed to take action and a number of search parties were organised with Colonel Georgy Ortyukov in overall charge. Colonel Ortyukov was head of UPI's Military Department, where members of the Dyatlov group had been well known and had numerous friends who were all by now deeply concerned at the delay in their return.

Once the decision was taken to undertake a search, there is no doubt that a considerable amount of resources was put into the effort, as with each day that passed with no news from the group it was becoming apparent that all was not well. Several rescue parties went north on 21 February. Two of the search parties included members of Yury Blinov's group who had just returned from the same mountains. Also involved were the Sogrin group, who also knew the members of the Dyatlov party and had also just returned from the area. These particular two search parties were experienced and knew the region well. A group headed by Vaselin Karelin, which was already in the area, also joined in the search. In addition to this, a major boost was given to the search by the use of aircraft and helicopters from Ivdel Airport. The airport itself was very small and used mainly by aircraft connected with the Gulag administration at Ivdel, but it had communications facilities and provided a reasonably close base for the two military helicopters and the civil helicopter provided by Aeroflot (the state airline), which were brought in to assist with the search. A light aircraft normally used to search for forest fires (a Yak 12) and an Aeroflot An-2 biplane were also deployed in the search. Although the An-2 had only a single propeller, it was a rugged workhorse that could operate in and out of rough strips and carry twelve passengers, along with equipment and supplies.

Among the concerned friends of the group at the university, there were enough volunteers to form another three search parties, which eventually came under the leadership of three individuals: Oleg Grebennik, Moses Akselrod and Boris Slobtsov.

On 22 February a search party formed by prison guards from the Ivdel Gulag joined in the search under the command of Captain A.A. Chernischev. This was in addition to a group of seven Ivdel policemen, led by Lieutenant Potapov. There was some irony in the Ivdel Gulag guards joining in the search, as one of the later theories (see Chapter 6) centres on the Dyatlov group being murdered by escaped prisoners from the Ivdel Gulag, which was the nearest prison camp to Kholat Syakhl.

In addition, local Mansi hunters who knew the area well also joined in the search. Although the Mansi had their own lives to get on with, their knowledge of the area surpassed that of any outsiders and, despite the theory that the Mansi may have murdered the group (see Chapter 6), the evidence does not appear to support this. One Mansi family in particular (whose family name was Kurikov) helped considerably by using their dogs in the search.

One of the three parties led by Boris Slobtsov (from UPI) was nominated to start their search near the base of Mount Otorten. Slobtsov was a close friend of Igor Dyatlov and three years previously had assisted him in making the tent that the Dyatlov group were using: they had basically stitched two tents together in order to double the capacity of the interior. It seemed logical to start one search party at the Dyatlov group's original final destination and then work backwards to look for signs of their return journey. A helicopter dropped Boris Slobtsov and his team off near the base of Mount Otorten on 23 February. It took them until the following day to reach the summit of Mount Otorten.

Once they reached the summit, Slobtsov and his party could find no evidence that the Dyatlov group had made it that far. Slobtsov had expected to see either a flag or some marker as evidence that the group had reached their goal. Not only was there no marker but there was no evidence of any tracks. The search party then started to make their way back in the direction in which Slobtsov had expected the Dyatlov group to make their approach to Mount Otorten. At this point it should be remembered that the group had pitched their tent 9 miles (15km) to the south of Mount Otorten on the pass at Kholat Syakhl, which was not necessarily on a direct route to their destination, but the Slobtsov search party was heading down from Mount Otorten back in the direction towards the River Auspia where Slobtsov assumed Dyatlov and his group would have come from. As Slobtsov's search party made their way the following day (25 February), they came across ski tracks that they quickly identified as belonging to the Dyatlov group.

On 26 February, after following the ski tracks, they came across the Dyatlov group's abandoned tent at the pass on the slopes of Kholat Syakhl. Although the tent was partially collapsed, Slobtsov recognised it straight away as the tent he had helped put together. The search party also immediately saw that there was no one there and that the tent appeared to have been abandoned.

The tent stood at a distance of less than 1,000ft (300m) from the summit of Kholat Syakhl. The angle of the mountain slope was eighteen to twenty degrees. An initial examination of the tent showed that the location had been selected correctly and provided good shelter. The tent was stretched on skis and ski poles pushed into the snow. Its entrance faced south and the tension ropes on the southern side were intact, but on the northern side they were broken and this part of the tent was partially under snow, brought by the February winter storms.

Part of the problem in trying to piece together what had happened is that no attempt was made to preserve the scene as it was found. No one at this stage thought that anything untoward had happened to the group. While the scene of the abandoned tent must have caused some concern, it was assumed that the group (who were all fit and well experienced in this type of environment) must have had good reasons for leaving the tent. As a result of the initial assessment of the scene, further confusion was caused by removal of articles from inside the tent. Also footsteps and tracks made by the search party added to the tracks that had been made by the group, further adding to the confusion. The actual tracks that were found leading away from the tent unfortunately became very quickly intermingled with the tracks made by the search party. The first assessment was that eight or nine tracks led away from the tent and down the slope of the mountain for a distance of roughly one-third of a mile (500m). These tracks were shown to have been made by people wearing no shoes and had character-istic 'columns' of pressed snow around where the indenta-tions had been made by the footprint. What members of the search party deduced was that the eight or nine tracks led down the slope in single file, with a tall man at the back; occasionally a track would wander out from the main file and would then return as if either wandering or looking for something. This would lead to a further question later: if the group felt they were in mortal danger and had slashed their way out of the tent to escape as quickly as possible, then why did they make what appeared to be such an orderly single-file descent down the slope at what appears to have been walking pace? The photos taken of the tracks, whilst not clear, show the paces taken to be fairly close to each other, rather than wild running strides, which would have left more of a scattered footprint.

What was found by Slobtsov's search party must have added to a growing sense of unease. As has already been mentioned, the side of the tent had been slashed open by knives for the group to get out rather than use the front entrance. There were several slashes on the side of the tent, with two large holes that were big enough for a person to get through. Although the stove that Dyatlov had designed was placed near the entrance, it was in a stowed position and not in use at the time of the group making their exit from the tent. Even if the stove had made it awkward for them to get out, the first main question by anybody observing the scene must have been: what had happened to cause the group to slash their way out of the tent and basically destroy it, in order to make their exit?

The next item to give cause for concern was the fact that inside the tent the search party found warm clothes, weatherproof jackets and pants plus footwear, along with flashlights and other implements such as knives. Some of the clothing was stacked around the edge in preparation for sleeping and other items were strewn on the ground sheet. There were also crumpled blankets, which lay in a frozen heap. Approximately 30–50ft (10–15m) away from the tent were found shoes, socks and Igor Dyatlov's fur jacket lying in the snow. A weatherproof jacket also lay nearby. All these items would be needed for survival in the harsh Siberian winter. Not to even take sweaters to keep warm must have raised serious questions about what had happened. On top of the tent, Slobtsov found a torch of Chinese make. It was lying on 1–3.5in (5–10cm) of snow but had no snow on it and was in working condition.

Shortly after the tent's discovery, the personal belongings of the group were removed. These included three cameras, diaries, clothes, shoes, cooking utensils, knives, hatchets and ski equipment, along with some alcohol and a 'joke' newspaper that the group had compiled, called the *Evening Otorten*, and which described their adventure. The last date on the *Evening Otorten* was 1 February 1959. This was the last day they were alive, but there is some dispute over this date as no diary entry was made. However, the whereabouts of the newspaper is unknown, so the date cannot be verified.

The removal of the items was done without any attempt at order and methodology, which only added to the questions of what had happened that night. One of the items removed was a damaged ski pole, which has been the subject of controversy as none of the group were known to have a ski pole which had been damaged by having cutting marks made on it. There was no obvious explanation for the pole, i.e. how it had got there, or how and why it was damaged.

After the discovery of the tent, Slobtsov and his party returned as quickly as they could to the base of the mountain, where a camp had been established, to report their find. A radioman named Igor Nevolin had joined the search parties and he radioed back to Sverdlovsk at 6 p.m. on the evening of 26 February to report the discovery of the tent. The response from UPI was that further help would be sent and, accordingly, a larger search party arrived by helicopter, along with two large military tents to provide more accommodation. Arriving with the larger search party was Colonel Georgy Ortyukov from UPI, who was in overall charge. In addition, further Mansi hunters and their dogs arrived to join in the search.

Once the military tents had been erected, the search parties took stock of the situation and planned the next phase of the search. Some comfort was taken in the fact that the Dyatlov group's money and rail tickets had been found in the tent with their belongings, which they took as a sign that no robbery had been involved in their disappearance, as these items would certainly have been taken. Prior to the search resuming, a meal was cooked for everyone and Boris Slobtsov proposed a toast to the health of his missing friends, saying that he hoped they soon would be found well. At this stage, it seemed impossible that all nine members of the group would have met their end; thus the mood of the searchers was optimistic. Another member of the party, Ivan Paschin, responded to Slobtsov's toast rather morbidly, saying that they should be drinking to the dead rather than the living, as he did not expect any of the Dyatlov group to be found alive. This statement drew a strong response from some of the students present, who expected to find their friends alive. A number of the students became aggressive towards Paschin, with a near-fight breaking out before tempers were calmed.

The discovery of the first two bodies seemed to happen almost by chance. On the morning of 27 February, two members of the main search party, Yury Koptelov and Michael Sharavin, were looking for a new spot for a campsite before resuming the search. They approached the River Lozva and noticed that there was a tall cedar tree nearby that had an area of flat land around it, which also gave a good view of the surrounding area and the mountain (Kholat Syakhl). The snow was not very thick in this area due to the effect of the wind. They approached the cedar to get a better look at the ground and vicinity and, as they came nearer, they noticed two bodies lying in the snow. These were the bodies of George Krivonischenko and Yury Doroshenko. They lay side by side, almost stripped to their underwear as well as having bare feet. Near to the bodies was the remains of a fire in which there were the tops of small trees, which had been cut with a knife. It was later deduced that George Krivonishchenko and Yury

Doroshenko must have tried to keep the fire going as long as they could (believed to be a period of one to one and a half hours) but it was not sufficient to warm them enough in the freezing conditions. There were burn marks on their hands and feet, which were believed to have been caused when they put their frostbitten feet and hands into the fire to warm them but did not feel the pain. They basically had frozen to death. The cedar tree was almost 1 mile (about 1,500m) from the tent and the branches had been broken to a height of approximately 13–16ft (4–5m). It looked as though members of the group had climbed the tree and broken off the branches to make the fire, as well as using a knife to cut smaller sections. Pieces of skin from one or more members of the group had also been found on the tree, where they had scraped themselves while climbing up.

As more members of the search party arrived at the scene, the Ivdel prosecutor, Vasily Tempalov, who was also involved in the search, found another body at a point roughly around 1,000ft (300m) from the cedar tree. Students in the search party quickly recognised the body of the group leader, Igor Dyatlov. He was lying on his back with his head pointing in the direction of their tent. Mansi hunters and their dogs then started to explore the mountainside of Kholat Syakhl and fairly quickly found the body of Zina Kolmogorova. It was actually one of the Mansi dogs (a German shepherd named Alma) who found her body, as she was covered by a 4in (10cm) layer of snow. She was found approximately one-third of a mile (500m) from the other three bodies and, like Igor Dyatlov, her body was pointing in the direction of the tent. It can be inferred that these four members of the group (George Krivonischenko, Yury Doroshenko, Igor Dyatlov and Zina Kolmogorova) had all been together near the cedar tree and had started a small fire. It is also interesting to note that Igor Dyatlov and Zina Kolmogorova, who were romantically linked, had stayed together and appear to have both attempted to make their way back to the tent. A possible explanation for the wide separation in where their bodies were found could be that they must have realised by this stage that their lives were in mortal danger, with the fire possibly having gone out, and had tried to make their own way back to the tent in a final desperate attempt to save themselves.

The search continued for another week with no sign of the remaining five members of the group (Rustem Slobodin, Luda Dubinina, Semyon Zolotarev, Nicolai Thibeaux-Brignolle and Alexander Kolevatov). What was found in the immediate area was another Chinese-made torch of the same type that had been found on top of the tent. The batteries were flat and the switch was still in the 'on' position. If this torch was being used by some of the group, then it was either thrown away as the elements overcame them, or the batteries went flat and it was just discarded.

On 2 March a search party composed of three UPI students and several Mansi hunters found a base camp in the valley of the Auspia River that had been left by the Dyatlov group. This store had been established by the group in order to ease their climb up the mountain. Once they had started their ascent, the going had become much harder and they were already carrying a good deal of equipment including the tent, stove and other accessories. The search party found approximately 120lb (55kg) of food, equipment (including a pair of skis and ski shoes), clothes and also Rustem Slobodin's mandolin. It was considered significant that all the items were still in place, particularly the food, which implied that the group were not being watched by anyone (particularly escaped prisoners) intent on stealing anything.

On 3 March, the students in the search parties had to return to Sverdlovsk to resume their studies. By this time many of them had been searching for almost two weeks. Two days after they had left, the body of Rustem Slobodin was found. An indication of how difficult the search must have been is that Slobodin's body was found in a line between the cedar and the tent, lying almost halfway between the bodies of Zina Kolmogorova and Igor Dyatlov. His body was very close by, but had gone unseen due to the snow. He was approximately 600ft (180m) ahead of Igor Dyatlov and 500ft (150m) behind Zina Kolmogorova (distances are approximate), as if they had all tried to crawl one after another in a line back to the tent. Slobodin's body is the only one that was warm when he fell, as the heat from his body had melted the snow beneath him, which had then frozen to form a kind of bed for his body. Slobodin's watch read 8.45 although it is not necessarily a significant time as watches in the 1950s had to be wound up to keep going – and it is possible the watch continued working after he had died, or it may have stopped before he died if he had not bothered to wind it up because he was too busy trying to stay alive.

It was to be almost two months later, on 4 May, before the remaining four members of the group were found, approximately 230ft (70m) away from the cedar tree. Their bodies were found beneath 13–15ft (4–4.5m) of snow. There does not seem to be any reason as to why the group appears to have split in two, a distance of 230ft (70m) apart from each other. Possibly they had tried to dig a hole in the deep snow as a form of shelter, with George Krivonischenko and Yury Doroshenko perhaps climbing the cedar tree to look back in the direction of the tent, assuming something had happened there, and also to get wood to make a fire.

The bodies of Luda Dubinina, Alexander Kolevatov, Semyon Zolotarev and Nicolai Thibeaux-Brignolle were all found together, some with serious internal injuries, including broken bones (Rustem Slobodin was found to have a fractured skull). This group of four had managed to create a shelter in a hollow in an attempt to keep warm by using branches, twigs and some clothes to form a kind of den. Luda Dubinina was found to be wearing clothes taken off Krivonischenko and Doroshenko (who were found almost naked). The clothes had been cut with a knife, evidently giving the appearance that they had been removed from the dead bodies of Krivonischenko and Doroshenko. Two of the sweaters found on the bodies were later found to contain levels of radiation.

A suggestion was made that all the members of the group should be buried at the mountain pass, which was to bear Igor Dyatlov's name. This was amended to possible burial in the town of Ivdel, before it was finally decided to bury them in Sverdlovsk. Seven of the group (Igor Dyatlov, Luda Dubinina, Zina Kolmogorova, Rustem Slobodin, Yury Doroshenko, Alexander Kolevatov and Nicolai Thibeaux-Brignolle) were buried in Mikhailovskoe Cemetery in a ceremony attended by hundreds of people. Many students from UPI attended, despite being instructed to avoid the ceremony and attend their lectures. It is felt that the authorities were doing their best to try to keep the funerals as low-key as possible.

George Krivonischenko and Semyon Zolotarev were both buried in Ivanoskoye Cemetery. It is said that this particular cemetery was closed at the time and there must have been reasons why these two burials took place there, rather than with the rest of the group. One reason given is that the two were somehow linked to the KGB. However, Krivonischenko's mother had connections within the authorities and she wanted her son buried at Ivanoskoye Cemetery instead of Mikhailovskoe. Zolotarev is considered by some to be a more shadowy figure and there may be other reasons why he was buried in this cemetery. He was also the last of the group to be buried. Krivonischenko's mother and relatives built the small concrete and brick wall around Zolotarev's grave as no one from his family had attended the burial or attended to the grave.

Criminal Case

A criminal investigation had been started to try and get to the bottom of what had happened. This investigation is the cause of much controversy. The man in charge was Lev Ivanov. After his retirement, he eventually went to live in Kazakhstan and his personal view was that there was a UFO involvement in the deaths of the Dyatlov group. He died in the 1990s but never deviated from his views. One of the oddest aspects about Ivanov's initial involvement at the pass on Kholat Syakhl was that he used a Geiger counter to take measurements of radiation shortly after the discovery of the tent and the bodies. It appears inexplicable that a policeman would feel the need to see whether radiation was present in what was initially considered to be possibly an open and shut case of misadventure, with people dying of hypothermia in blizzard conditions. Whether there was official sanction for it or whether he was using his own initiative is not known. A Geiger counter would not be part of a normal policeman's investigative tools in the Soviet Union of 1959, but it may have been given to him by the authorities as part of the investigation, which itself raises the question of why the authorities felt the need for the presence of radiation to be measured in the vicinity.

The area was closed off completely for four years by the authorities and not reopened until 1963. On its reopening, a memorial plaque to the members of the Dyatlov group was fixed to a large rock at the pass, which was renamed Dyatlov Pass in memory of the dead ski tourists.

The following is an extract from the conclusions of the investigation and the final decision to terminate the criminal case:

Considering the lack on the dead bodies of external injuries and signs of struggle, the presence in place of all group's valuables, and also taking into account the forensic report on the causes of death of the tourists, it shall be considered that death of the tourists had been caused by an elemental force which the tourists were unable to overcome.

Autopsies

One of the most unusual aspects of the autopsies was the lack of any external markings (not even scratches) to those in the group who had suffered the worst internal injuries. The first four bodies of the party to have autopsies performed on them were that of Yury Doroshenko, George Krivonischenko, Igor Dyatlov and Zina Kolmogorova. The autopsies were carried out by medical examiner Boris Vozrozhdenny and were performed in the village of Vizhay on 4 March 1959. Rustem Slobodin's autopsy was performed also in Vizhay on 8 March, shortly after his body was found. The remaining four bodies were not found until early May, with autopsies performed shortly afterwards.

Members of the families commented on the discolouration of the skin of the bodies, saying that some of them looked as if they had the skin of someone of African descent. Yury Kuntsevich of the Dyatlov Foundation was 12 years old at the time and attended the funerals. He recalled seeing the apparently 'deeply tanned skin' of the deceased.

George Krivonischenko

Krivonischenko's body was found under the same cedar tree as Yury Doroshenko. The findings of the autopsy were:

There were bruises on his forehead 0.3 x 1.8cm and there was a bruise around the left temporal bone.

Diffuse bleeding in the right temporal and occipital region due to damage to temporalis muscle.

Tip of nose missing.

Frostbitten ears.

Bruises on the right side of the chest 7 x 2cm and 2 x 1.2cm.

Bruises on hands.

Detachment of the epidermis on the back of the left hand to a width of 2cm.

Portion of the epidermis from the right hand was found in his mouth.

Bruises on the thighs with minor scratches.

Bruise on the left buttock 10 x 3cm.

Abrasions on the outer side of the left thigh 6.2cm and 4.5cm.

Bruises on the left leg 2 x 1cm, 2 x 1.5cm and 3 x 1.3cm.

Burn on the left leg 10 x 4cm.

There was 500g of urine in his bladder. The official cause of Krivonischenko's death was given as hypothermia. One aspect of his and Yury Doroshenko's freezing to death was the possibility of so-called 'paradoxical undressing' (see Chapter 6). Krivonischenko was found dressed in a long-sleeved shirt, swimming pants, pants and a torn sock on his left leg. He was not wearing any footwear.

Yury Doroshenko

Yury Doroshenko had frozen to death and was found along with George Krivonischenko, under the cedar tree where they had built a small fire. They were thought to have been the first of the group to die. The results of the autopsy were as follows:

Ear, nose and lips were covered in blood.

His right armpit had a bruise 2 x 1.5cm.

The inner surface of his right shoulder had two abrasions 2 x 1.5cm with no bleeding in the tissue. There were two cuts in the skin.

There were brown/red bruises on the upper third of his right forearm. These measured 4 x 1cm, 2.5 x 1.5cm and 5 x 5cm.

The fingers of both hands had torn skin.

There was bruised skin in the upper third of both legs.

There were signs of frostbite on his face and ears.

There were foamy grey fluid discharges on his right cheek, from the mouth.

There was 150g of urine in his bladder.

Much has been made by theorists of the foamy grey discharge from his mouth, which was found on his cheek. It has been speculated that this was caused by someone pressing on his chest. The official cause of Doroshenko's death was given as hypothermia. When he was found by the search party, he was wearing a vest, a shirt, a short-sleeved shirt, and knitted pants with a pair of shorts over these pants. The pants had tears on the inner thighs. He had no footwear but was wearing socks, of which the left sock was burnt. The issue of 'paradoxical undressing' in relation to Yury Doroshenko is referred to in Chapter 6.

Zinaida Kolmogorova

Zinaida Kolmogorova was found nearest to the tent, almost as though she was trying to get back to it, although she was still some considerable distance away, especially considering what must have been her very weak state at the end. The results of her autopsy were:

Swelling of Meninges. [The Meninges is the system of membranes that covers the central nervous system and their swelling was an important feature of hypothermia.[1]]

70

Frostbite on the phalanges of the fingers.
Numerous bruises on her hands and palms.
A long bruise that encircled her right side 29 x 6cm.
There was 300g of urine in her bladder.

The autopsy also showed that she was not sexually active at any time near her death. The cause of death was stated as hypothermia. When her body was found, Zina was wearing two hats, a long-sleeved shirt, a sweater, a second shirt and a second sweater with torn cuffs. It could not be determined whether she had cut off the second sweater or whether the damage had been done by someone else. In addition she was wearing trousers, cotton athletic pants, ski pants (with three small holes in the bottom), three pairs of socks and a military mask, but was not wearing any footwear. As she was wearing more clothing than the others, this may have accounted for the fact that, of the whole group, she was closest in what seemed to be an attempt to get back to the tent. Had she made it back there, her chances of survival would have increased considerably.

Igor Dyatlov

The body of the leader of the group was found approximately 1,000ft (300m) from the cedar tree. Like Zina, it appeared that he had been trying to return to the tent. The results of his autopsy were:

Dried blood on the lips.
There were numerous dark red scratches on the lower third of the right forearm and the palms of the hands.
There were brown/red bruises in the area of the Metacarpo-phalangeal joints of the right hand. A common injury in hand fights using fists.

There were brown/purple bruises on the left hand with superficial wounds on the 2nd and 5th fingers of the left hand. Minor abrasions on the forehead.

Abrasions above the left eyebrow of a brown/red colour.

Abrasions on both cheeks of a brown/red colour.

There was an incisor missing on the lower jaw but the mucosa was intact which suggested that the incisor was lost long before the final journey.

Both knees were bruised without bleeding into the underlying tissue.

There was bruising on the lower third of the right leg.

There were bright red abrasions on both ankles which were 1 x 0.5cm and 3.0 x 2.5cm with haemorrhage into the underlying tissue.

There were no internal injuries.

There was approximately one litre of urine in the bladder.

The cause of death was stated as hypothermia. Igor was wearing a sweater, a fur coat (with pockets) which had not been buttoned up, a long-sleeved shirt, and ski pants over his pants. He had no footwear but was wearing a cotton sock on his left foot and a woollen sock on his right foot. He was also bareheaded. Yury Yudin later stated that the long-sleeved shirt found on Igor Dyatlov belonged to him, and that he had originally given it to Yury Doroshenko when he left the group to return because of his illness. It can be deduced that Dyatlov had removed the shirt from the body of Doroshenko after he froze to death. Three items were also found on Dyatlov: a watch, which showed the time as 5.31, a pocketknife and a photograph of Zina Kolmogorova.

Rustem Slobodin
The body of the mandolin player Rustem Slobodin was found 500ft (150m) behind Zina Kolmogorova and 600ft

(180m) ahead of Igor Dyatlov. He was wearing one boot on his right foot, along with two shirts (one long-sleeved), two pairs of pants, four pairs of socks and a sweater. His watch had stopped at 8.45. He was carrying his passport, 310 rubles, a knife, pencil, pen, comb and matchbox. The results of the autopsy were:

Traces of blood discharge from the nose.

Swollen lips.

Swelling with a number of small, irregularly shaped abrasions on the right side of the face.

Minor brown/red abrasions on the forehead, two scratches 1.5cm long and 0.3cm apart.

A brown/red bruise on the upper eyelid of the right eye with haemorrhage into the underlying tissues.

Abrasions on the left side of the face.

The epidermis was torn from the right forearm.

[As with Igor Dyatlov] There were bruises in the area of the Metacarpophalangeal joints of both hands [only Dyatlov's right hand was so affected; a common injury in hand fights using fists.]

Brown/cherry coloured bruises on the medial aspect of the left arm and left palm.

Bruising on the left tibia measuring 2.5 x 1.5cm.

There was also identified a fracture of the frontal bone and haemorrhaging in the temporalis muscle of Rustem's skull. Despite some of the injuries he suffered, the cause of death was given as hypothermia. The skull fracture may have been caused by a fall or could have been caused by a blunt object hitting him. It was observed in the autopsy that the blow or fall that caused the skull fracture would have resulted in shock and a loss of co-ordination, which would have accelerated his death by hypothermia.

Lyudmila Dubinina

Belonging to the second group of bodies, Luda Dubinina was found close to the den that the second group had tried to create. She was in a kneeling position, lying against a rock by a stream. The injuries sustained by her were the worst and were almost inexplicable. Her tongue was stated as just being 'missing', along with the muscles of the floor of her mouth. The autopsy does not state that her tongue was torn out. There was 100g of coagulated blood in her stomach, which is taken to imply that her heart was beating and blood was flowing when her tongue was removed. The results of her autopsy were:

Tongue missing.

Soft tissue missing around the eyes, eyebrows and left temporal area with partially exposed bone.

Eyes missing.

Nose cartilage broken and flattened.

Four ribs were broken on the right side with two fracture lines visible.

Six ribs were broken with two fracture lines visible.

Soft tissue of the upper lip missing, teeth and upper jaw exposed.

Massive haemorrhage in the heart's right atrium.

Bruise in the middle left thigh measuring 10 x 5cm.

Damaged tissues around the left temporal bone measuring 4 x 4cm.

Luda was wearing two sweaters, two shirts – one with long sleeves and one with short sleeves, underwear, long socks plus two pairs of smaller socks and another single sock, plus a small hat. She was not wearing any footwear and in an attempt to protect her feet had cut a sweater in half and wrapped one half around her left foot. The other half of the sweater was found lying in the snow. Her cause of death was stated as haemorrhage into the right atrium of the heart, multiple fractured ribs and internal bleeding. Her fractures were symmetrical and are believed to be impossible to have been caused by falling onto rocks, quite apart from the lack of any external marks on the skin.

Semyon Zolotarev

Also in the second group found, the body of Semyon Zolotarev was found close to the den that this group had created. He too, like Luda Dubinina, had suffered serious and seemingly inexplicable internal injuries. The results of his autopsy were:

Eyeballs missing.

Missing soft tissue around the left eyebrow measuring 7 x 6cm with bone exposed.

Flair chest with five ribs broken on the right side with two fracture lines.

Open wound on the right side with exposed bone measuring 8 x 6cm.

Zolotarev was found to have three tattoos: on the back of his right wrist at the base of the thumb, a tattooed male name, GENA; on the back of the right forearm, a tattooed outline of a beetroot and the letter C; on the back of the left forearm, two Cyrillic letters, plus separately a combination of eleven Cyrillic letters and the number 3, a five-pointed star, four more Cyrillic letters and the year 1921. The year probably refers to his year of birth.

Alexander Kolevatov

Another member of the second group, the body of Alexander Kolevatov was found close to the den. The results of his autopsy were:

Lack of soft tissue around the eyes.

Eyebrows missing.

Skull bone exposed.

Broken nose.

Open wound behind the ear, size 3 x 1.5cm.

Deformed neck.

Intravital subluxation of the foot [which was bandaged with a piece of cloth].

Nicolai Thibeaux-Brignolle

The final member of the second group, the body of Nicolai Thibeaux-Brignolle was also found close to the den. The results of his autopsy were:

Multiple fractures to the temporal bone with extensions to the frontal and sphenoid bones.

Haemorrhage on the lower forearm measuring 10 x 12cm.

Bruise on the left side of the upper lip.

A fall of some kind onto a rock as the cause for the large and unusual skull fracture was dismissed at the autopsy, which leaves the question: what else could have caused the damage to his skull? Some of the theories about what caused the deaths may account for what caused the skull fracture (avalanche/ fight/attacks by criminals or special forces, etc), but whatever caused the damage must have happened fairly close to where he died, as he probably would have been unable to make his way from the tent without being carried or dragged. None of the evidence points to any member of the group being carried or dragged by the others.

6

What happened – official findings

This chapter looks at possible explanations using the official investigation as a guideline (particularly the only footprints present being from the group themselves) and also looks at all the possibilities arising from the deaths occurring in the vicinity of the tent and the lower slope of Kholat Syakhl by the tree line. The official investigation was concluded on 28 May 1959.

Fifty-one years after the tragedy, the Dyatlov Memorial Foundation organised a conference on 2 February 2010 at Ural State Technical University to bring a number of experts and interested parties together in order to try and answer some of the many questions surrounding this mystery. In the process, they examined a number of the main theories that have been put forward.

The following presents a list of possible scenarios that may have either directly caused the deaths of the group or been a significant contributory factor. All the possibilities suggested have been put forward at different times by different sources, ranging from the highly probable to the fantastic. There is also a line of thought supported by some that there is a simple and mundane explanation for the deaths. This line of thought is that they all left the tent and six of them froze to death; the other three (all three of them at the same time) fell into a ravine, seriously injuring themselves as they did so, and then were overcome by the elements. On the face of it, this is certainly plausible, but the following questions have to be asked: why did they slash the tent with knives to get out so quickly? What is mundane about nine experienced hikers/skiers leaving the confines of safety to walk or run to their certain deaths? Who in their right minds would commit virtual suicide as a group, unless someone or something had forced them to do so? Why did the group split into two and end up apart from each other? If they fell to their deaths in a ravine why did they all do so – did they follow each other over the edge and fall down one after another or did they all fall into a ravine at the same time? They cannot have been looking for help as they knew very well that they were many miles away from any help or civilisation. That is what takes this tragedy beyond the mundane.

Hypothermia and 'paradoxical undressing'

The fact that a number of the members of the group died from hypothermia cannot be disputed, assuming that one takes the autopsy results as correct (i.e. not falsified by pressure from outside influences). The first autopsies were held in Vizhay, which had the most basic of facilities, and it was the first five bodies – two of which were found near the cedar tree and the other three almost in a line possibly trying to get back to the tent – who were all found basically to have died from being exposed to the elements (i.e. died from the cold) and being inadequately clothed. The other four members of the group were not found until early May; three of this second group – Luda Dubinina, Semyon Zolotarev and Nicolai Thibeaux-Brignolle – had received serious internal injuries, the causes of which are unexplained. The hypothermia theory, which could also be called the mundane theory, posits that everyone froze to death with some of them falling and badly injuring themselves (although Luda Dubinina missing her tongue is not so easily explained in this scenario).

One theory put forward is that the group succumbed to the phenomenon known as 'paradoxical undressing' – the term used to describe people who are freezing to death and who start to remove the clothes that are keeping them warm, thereby hastening their deaths. It is assumed by some that paradoxical undressing had led to the deaths of many in the group. The supposition is that both George Krivonischenko and Yury Doroshenko were the first to die and that they both froze to death. They were both found by the search party in a state of undress and it could be taken that, in a delirious state, they both succumbed to the condition. However, this is not borne out by investigation. Some of the clothes they were wearing were found on the others (e.g. Luda Dubinina was wearing clothes belonging to Doroshenko and Krivonischenko) and had been removed after death, in some cases with the use of a knife. The bodies of Doroshenko and Krivonischenko were found side by side, which suggests that their bodies had been moved and placed in this position by the surviving members of the group – and showed respect for the two dead. What can be inferred from this – the removal of the clothes from the already dead members of the group – is that they had tried to keep as warm as possible with what they had.

The issue of paradoxical undressing is worth examining in detail but, as will be shown, it is a wrong assumption and not only that, but it does not adequately explain the events that took place that night.

Paradoxical undressing is a condition that is common in winter survival and is known in some Western mountaineering circles as 'cold stupid'. Whilst the term itself and the issue of hypothermia are commonly associated with mountaineering, it can occur wherever the danger of hypothermia arises. As an example, paradoxical undressing was present in thirty-three cases of deaths by hypothermia that had been collated by Swedish police in a study in 1979.[1] The cases had an even distribution of age, sex and geographic location, although it was found that most occurred between November and February in areas of open land (though some occurred in towns). Significantly, arteriosclerosis and chronic alcoholism were important concomitant illnesses, with alcoholism being a factor in many middle-aged men. Ethanol and other drugs were present in 67 per cent of the men and 78 per cent of the women, with ethanol predominating in the males and various psychotropic agents (tranquillisers, sedatives and antidepressants) in the females. The mean blood concentration that was found in the males was 0.16 per cent and in females 0.18 per cent. The most frequent findings at autopsy were purple spots or discolouration on the extremities, pulmonary edema (fluid accumulation in the lungs) and gastric haemorrhages.

Hypothermia occurs when the ambient temperature is below that of the body. If clothing also becomes wet, the cooling effect of evaporation also considerably increases the possibility of hypothermia occurring. It may seem totally illogical that a person suffering from hypothermia (i.e. freezing to death) would then start to remove their clothes and hasten their own deaths. There is, however, a physiological explanation for the strange behaviour.

In conditions of extreme cold, the body attempts to protect itself by moving blood away from the extremities and into the centre of the body (the core of the body) in order to protect the vital organs. This is why hands and feet become noticeably colder first while this is happening. The way that the movement of blood away from the extremities is achieved is by vasoconstriction of the peripheral circulation. Basically, the body is attempting to insulate the inner core by losing less heat. Vasoconstriction is the vascular contraction of the smooth muscles, and this effort of contraction requires a steady input of energy, which is in the form of glucose from the body's energy stores. However, due to the lack of blood flowing to these muscles, they eventually tire and a process known as vasodilation takes place. They then relax and start to open up. With vasodilation taking place in these blood vessels (i.e. opening up) there is an infusion of warm blood from the core of the body going to the peripheral extremities, which were cold up to this point. This has the effect of creating a feeling of excessive warmth in the victim, who is already well on the way to dying of hypothermia. Once the victim starts feeling much warmer because of this flow of warm blood to their extremities, they start to shed their clothes, thereby speeding up the process of the body temperature lowering.

By the time paradoxical undressing occurs, the person is in serious danger of dying from hypothermia. In mountaineering, there are no known examples where anyone who has reached this stage has survived without outside intervention. In fact persons suffering from the condition have been known to push away or refuse attempts to warm them when they are being helped.

Another condition related to hypothermia is known as 'terminal burrowing behaviour',[2] which is allied to paradoxical undressing (also referred to in a 1978–94 study as the 'so-called Paradox Reaction', i.e. undressing[3]). With 'terminal burrowing behaviour', an autonomous process of the brain stem triggers a primitive, burrowing-like behaviour for protection, similar to that found in hibernating animals. This is in the final stage of hypothermia. It is essentially a final attempt by the body to save itself and is followed by

unconsciousness and death. In the 1978–94 study of terminal burrowing behaviour in relation to hypothermia, it was
found that the deaths had occurred mainly with compara-
tively slow drops in body temperature and moderately cold
conditions, which would not have applied in the Dyatlov
case. There appears to have been an attempt by the second
group of four (Luda Dubinina, Semyon Zolotarev, Nicolai
Thibeaux-Brignolle and Alexander Kolevatov) to attempt to
build a shelter using twigs in a hollowed-out area of snow.
However, rather than exhibiting any kind of 'burrowing
behaviour', this appears more likely to have been a quite
rational attempt to build some kind of a shelter from the
worst of the elements. The lack of footwear on all members
of the group shows the extreme panic and alarm that the
members of the group must have experienced when leaving the tent, rather than the effects of the cold making them
leave their footwear behind.

The theory that at least George Krivonischenko and
Yury Doroshenko fell victim to paradoxical undressing
and started removing their clothes does not explain why
they had allowed themselves to reach this stage in the first
place. The body starts to freeze before paradoxical undressing starts, so why did they not return to the comparative
safety of the tent to at least try to keep warm? If they could
not find their way back to the tent because of the darkness,
or if they feared something close to the tent (see avalanche
below), the theory of paradoxical undressing whilst possibly
explaining some of the deaths does not explain what caused
them to run away from the tent in the first place. As already
stated, whilst both Doroshenko and Krivonischenko were
found without most of their clothes, these clothes were later
found on Luda Dubinina with cut marks on them, which
suggests they had been removed from Doroshenko and
Krivonischenko after they had died – by those left alive and

trying to keep warm. The issue of paradoxical undressing does not therefore apply in the case of what happened to the members of the Dyatlov group.

Avalanche

There are two aspects to the avalanche theory. The first is that the tent was hit by an actual avalanche; the second is that they feared they were about to be hit by an avalanche, causing them to exit the tent in a panic and get away from it as fast as possible. This would explain why they went down the slope of Kholat Syakhl rather than upwards or to the sides.

An avalanche is a sudden, drastic flow of snow down a slope and is caused by a trigger that can either be a natural one such as rain or more snow, or an artificial trigger, which can vary widely from skiers travelling over the surface, snowmobiles, snowboarders, explosives, loud sounds or even movement by animals or groups of animals.

Generally speaking, gravity acts on uncompacted newly fallen snow or on older snow that may be thawing. Air and water can mix with the snow as it moves and the avalanche, if it is large enough, can devastate everything before it, including trees and buildings, as well of course as killing anyone in its path. Avalanches are not particularly rare; there is always the possibility they could occur wherever there is packed snow in mountains.

Avalanches are classified by their characteristics, which include the cause of the avalanche itself, the type of snow, the nature of the failure, the sliding surface, the slope angle, the slope aspect and its elevation. Slopes flatter than twenty-five degrees or greater than sixty degrees generally have a lower incidence of avalanche. Human-triggered avalanches have the greatest incidence when the snow's angle of repose is between thirty-five and forty-five degrees. The critical angle at which human-triggered avalanches are most frequent is thirty-eight degrees. It can generally be said that a slope that is flat enough to hold snow but steep enough to ski has the potential to cause an avalanche, regardless of the angle.[4] The slope directly above the Dyatlov group's tent was eighteen to twenty degrees.

One suggestion is that there was an avalanche that only hit part of the tent, causing the worst of the injuries to Luda Dubinina, Semyon Zolotarev and Nicolai Thibeaux-Brignolle.[5] The remainder of the group slashed their way out of the tent and then helped their injured friends to the tree line as they feared another avalanche may have been about to hit them and cover the tent completely, which explains their rush to escape without adequate clothing and footwear. While the lack of heavy snow cover on the tent could be partially explained by wind blowing away the snow, many feel that there was no real evidence to suggest there was any kind of an avalanche.

The possibility must therefore be considered that they feared they were about to be hit by an avalanche and, in the dark and confusion, this would also possibly explain why they did not return to the tent fairly quickly to try and recover clothing and footwear or even to attempt to patch up the tent and settle back inside to better protect themselves from the elements. The bodies were found some distance away (the cedar tree and den they created were in the region of almost 1 mile or 1,500m) from the tent, so in the event of an avalanche it can be assumed they may have felt they were far enough away from the tent for safety. It is also a possibility that the darkness would not have enabled them to either find their way back to the tent by trying to retrace their footsteps (assuming they could see them) or to have enabled them to make an objective assessment as to the likelihood of a potential avalanche. Initially, as they were all in the tent and could not see out, it can be assumed that if they feared an avalanche they would have heard a noise first that caused them to panic. The place where they pitched their tent on the slope of Kholat Syakhl was not excessively steep – more to the point, they were less than 1,000 feet (300m) from the top of the mountain, so there would not have been enough space for a large quantity of snow to build up to cause a serious avalanche. The snow was only just over 3ft deep (1m). Igor Dyatlov had recorded the snow covering at 1.22m on 31 January – the last recorded entry in the group diary. This was not excessive for the area and time of year, although the previous day's entry (30 January) had mentioned how cold it was and gave the night time temperature as -26°C. A strong wind was also blowing, which reduced the temperature further.

From a physical point of view, the tent had not been crushed by an avalanche and was not completely buried under snow. Even if this had been the case, there had been no reason for them all to run away from the tent so far and to stay away so long. The Dyatlov group were all highly experienced in these conditions and unlikely to have behaved in such a manner as to put their lives at risk if there had only been a small avalanche. Also, the broken bones in three of them are not the sort of injuries they would have been expected to receive by an avalanche hitting the tent.

Military accident

The whole of the countryside immediately east of the Ural Mountains could be described as one vast military area. The production of armaments and military equipment, which was moved out of the range of Nazi bombing attacks during the Second World War, mainly stayed where it was and in most cases was expanded in order to meet the demands of the Cold War.

Ground forces (regular army)

Whilst the bulk of the Soviet ground forces were stationed well to the west of the Urals, facing NATO – notably in what came to be known as the Western Strategic Direction in the event of war with NATO – there were still sizeable concentrations of ground forces spread around the rest of the USSR, including the Ural Military District with its headquarters in Sverdlovsk. Despite the presence of what appeared to be a military testing area in a mountain area known as Chistop, close to where the Dyatlov group were making their trip, it was generally not an area used by the army or ground forces. It has been denied by the military authorities that this (the Chistop mountain area) was used for any kind of testing. However, old pieces of military equipment have been found in the area, including what appears to be small missile parts, sections of fuel tanks and pieces of radar equipment. Despite the presence of a possible testing area on the Chistop massif, areas used by the military for exercises are designated closed areas, known as Polygons. Even though it would have been possible to enter one (on account of the sheer size of some of them), the planned route for the Dyatlov group was not one of these closed areas, and the area was also regularly used by the Mansi for hunting and herding deer. Even allowing for a possible army training exercise on Kholat Syakhl to have taken place and gone wrong, there was no evidence at the scene of blast damage or shell fragments etc, or of large numbers of tracks that would be expected if an army unit had been there at the time. This does not rule out this type of accident having taken place elsewhere such as Chistop (see Chapter 7, Thermobaric weapons, and also Special forces).

Air force

Many commentators have stated that the nearest airbase was close to Sverdlovsk, almost 372 miles (600km) away. However, there was an airbase that was only one-third of this distance away. Yugorsk Sovetsky airbase (also known as Pionerskiy, Komsomolskiy-2 and Yugorsk-2) lay 125 miles (202km) to the south-east of the Kholat Syakhl pass. It became operational in 1952 with the formation of an Interceptor Aviation Regiment, 763 IAP, in June that year. The base was finally closed in 1998. In 1959 it was home to one squadron of Yak-25M (NATO codename Flashlight-A) and two squadrons of MiG-17 (NATO codename Fresco) fighter aircraft. The long-range Yak-25M Flashlight-A had a range of 2,560km (1,600 miles) and the MiG-17 Fresco had a range of 2,060km (1,290 miles), so Kholat Syakhl was well within the range of these aircraft, and regular missions were flown over the northern Ural Mountains. The function of 763 IAP was air defence of the northern Urals region, which in reality meant that in the event of a war breaking out with NATO, their primary task was the interception of the American bombers of Strategic Air Command coming in to attack from the direction of the Polar icecap.

As these aircraft of 763 IAP regularly flew over the northern Urals, one of the theories is that one or more aircraft flew close to the Dyatlov group tent. The engines of both types of aircraft made a considerable noise (the MiG-17 Frescos had afterburners) and it is suggested that one or more aircraft may have flown relatively low over the area where the group were camped; the shock may have forced them out of the tent quickly as they did not know what had caused the sound. However, there is a possibility that they may have feared the loud noise setting off a potential avalanche. These were early interceptors without the highly sophisticated computerised flying systems of the twenty-first century and it is very unlikely that these air-craft would have been flying too low at night in a mountain-ous region. However, even at height the engines made a loud noise audible at ground level. The sound of these types of engine make a low rumbling noise from some distance away and a variation of the theory is that the low rumbling of one or more overflying aircraft may have been mistaken by the party inside the tent for the start of an avalanche. They may have slashed their way out of the tent to find that they could not see or hear any more, which could have made them think that an avalanche was starting and so they took the decision to get away from the tent just in case. Nevertheless, despite the wish to get away from the tent as fast as possible, it would have been thought that they would at least have made sure they were pro-tected against the elements.

Neither the Yak-25M Flashlight-A nor the MiG-17 Fresco aircraft operated by 763 IAP carried bombs; they were purely interceptor aircraft. (See Chapter 7 for Tu-95 air mines.)

Rockets and missiles[6]

One theory is that the group were victims of the test firing of a missile or rocket, which had either passed very close to them or landed and exploded not far away. This theory is tied in with the theory regarding 'lights' or 'light orbs' in the night skies around the area (see below).

After the Second World War great effort was put into research and production of all types of missiles, with the emphasis on long-range missiles tipped with nuclear war-heads, which become known as ICBMs (Intercontinental Ballistic Missiles). Using captured German scientists and a substantial amount of captured German V2 technology, a large area in the Astrakhan region near to Volgograd at Kapustin Yar was established to develop, research and launch new missiles. In 1955 another large site was also established at Baikonur in Kazakhstan (referred to by the Americans as Tyuratam) to test ICBMs and also carry out associated space research.

In 1959 the later Space Cosmodrome at Plesetsk in the Archangelsk Oblast (region) had only recently been established as a military base (with the Russian code name Angara) for the R-7 Semyorka ICBM. There were several rough groups of rockets and missiles used by the Soviet military in 1959, including strategic missiles of various ranges, air-to-air and air-to-surface missiles, surface-to-air missiles; naval missiles and army rockets (including tactical anti-tank weapons). For the purposes of any relevance to the Dyatlov mystery, most of these can be discounted.

Naval missiles were only just being developed. These were tested at sea (initially the Black Sea), although examples were fired from sea to ranges on land, but the northern Urals contained no ranges for these sea-launched missiles. The first anti-ship missile, P-15 Termit (NATO codenamed SS-N-2 Styx), only had a range of 24 miles (40km). Similarly air-to-air missiles were in a fairly early stage of development. The area was regularly overflown by the MiG-17 Frescos and Yak-25M Flashlight-As of 763 IAP at Yugorsk Sovetsky (see Air force, above); in 1959, however, these aircraft had 37mm cannon fitted as their standard offensive armament.

The use of army rockets (including anti-tank missiles) would have been possible. However, it was not an area known for the use of these types of weapons by the army and neither was it used for army exercises in this period.

This leaves two main possibilities, which are regularly suggested in connection with the Dyatlov incident: surface-to-air missiles and ICBMs.

Surface-to-air missiles

The S-75 Dvina system (NATO codename SA-2 Guideline) was the missile that brought down the U-2 spy aircraft flown by Gary Powers near Sverdlovsk on 1 May 1960. The S-75 was deployed from 1957 onwards. This highly successful anti-aircraft missile was deployed in batteries, which although were mobile in that everything could be disassembled in one place and reassembled in another place fairly quickly, they were complex systems that worked in conjunction with radar and thus would be better described as located on semi-static sites. Mention has been made on some websites that a 'Dvina missile' may have been responsible for what happened to the Dyatlov group, but it is extremely unlikely: by early 1959 the testing phase of the initial missile type was over and, in any event, testing was first carried out near to the plants where they were made, notably at the Rzhevka site near the Leningrad (now St Petersburg) production plant. Final testing of these missiles was carried out at Kapustin Yar in Kazakhstan. When the S-75 was deployed, the batteries were located close to possible targets that could be attacked from the air, i.e. cities, manufacturing plants, military installations. They were also placed along the possible routes that it was expected an air attack might come from – either the United States or other NATO forces in the West. There were numerous batteries in the Sverdlovsk region as there were many targets of value there. However, the main point about these missiles is that the first models only had a range of 13 to 14 miles (22 to 24km). For the Dyatlov group to have been close to one of these falling to the ground with its explosive warhead, they would have had to have been within range of a launch site. There is no evidence of such a launch site at the time in the area. As testing was complete on the missiles by 1959, there was no requirement to take them to such an awkward location and test them and, added to which, given their range of only 13 to 14 miles (22 to 24km), there was nothing there for them to protect. It is possible that the place where the Dyatlov group were found at Kholat Syakhl could have fallen under the route of a possible air attack by US bomber aircraft coming in over the Polar icecap, but for an S-75 site to be established it would have required considerable logistics to set it up in such an awkward location and it would have been virtually impossible to conceal its presence from people in the area.

ICBMs

The only ICBM in use by the Soviet Union in 1959 was the R-7 Semyorka, which was only becoming operational in 1958–59 with an estimated ten operational examples. Test firings of this ICBM began in August 1957 and up to 1959 there were approximately twenty test firings. Without exception, all of them were fired from the rangehead at Baikonur and landed 3,500 miles away in the impact area in the Kamchatka peninsula, i.e. in a completely different eastward direction to the location of the Dyatlov group. There were some failures of these test launches but none of them went anywhere near the Urals. There is, however, one unsubstantiated reference to the launch of an R-7 from the Angara military base at Plesetsk on 9 February 1959.[7] This is highly relevant, but as it was an operational military matter (i.e. the launch of an ICBM from a military site), checking its veracity is another matter. The official acceptance of the R-7 into military service was announced in a decree on 20 January 1960 but several examples were operational before then. The later (from 1960) military derivative of the R-7, the R-7A, was given the NATO codename SS-6 Sapwood.

The theory that a test firing from Baikonur of a ballistic missile that went astray was partially laid to rest by an article

about the Dyatlov group deaths in a local Ekaterinburg newspaper *Oblastnaya Gazeta* dated 30 January 1999. In an article
entitled 'Already Forty Years' it was stated:

> In the period under consideration (between 25 January to 5
> February 1959) no launches of ballistic missiles or space rockets
> were made from the Baikonur Cosmodrome. The north Urals
> is located many hundreds of kilometres away from missile
> lanes. We assert unambiguously that no falls of a rocket or its
> fragments is possible in the area in question.

At first sight, what is stated in this article appears to be borne
out by examining the lists of launches that were made. The
R-7 Semyorka with the nearest launch dates took place on 24
December 1958 (recorded as a failure) and 17 March 1959. No
reference is made in the article to the launch of an R-7 in military service at Angara, Plesetsk on 9 February 1959.

It is also worth considering the launch of intermediate range missiles from Kapustin Yar. Kholat Syakhl was
just beyond the official range of these missiles. However, an
R-5M was actually launched from the test site at Kapustin
Yar on 2 February 1959. The R-5M was an intermediate range weapon with a maximum range of 1,200km
(745 miles) and the Dyatlov group were beyond its range
as they were 1,700km (1,060 miles) away to the north-east.
The R-5M test launches had ranges of between 1,083km
(672 miles) and 1,200km (745 miles) aimed towards a point
near Priaralsk Karakum, 150 miles north-east of the Aral
Sea. There appears to have been no launch of a 1,500km
R-12 (NATO codename SS-4 Sandal) and the nearest date
examples of this missile launch were 30 December 1958 and
30 March 1959.

Despite this launch of the R-5M on 2 February 1959,
what is stated in the article extract above is true – that the

northern Urals was hundreds of kilometres from missile test lanes and that nothing was launched from Baikonur between the relevant dates of the Dyatlov group trip, allowing for the unsubstantiated launch of the R-7 from Angara, Plesetsk on 9 February 1959.

There is mention in a few studies of the Dyatlov incident of rockets with sodium trails being observed in the northern Urals, with the launches having taken place in the Kola Peninsula with the impact area located in the Tyumen Oblast in the Arctic Urals. This had first been suggested in a letter to a Moscow newspaper by Alexsey Koskin, an engineer and tourist who had visited the pass many times. He said that the 'lights' which were observed were sodium trails from these rockets, which were testing satellites and were coming down in the Nadym test field hundreds of kilometres to the north-east of Kholat Syakhl. The suggestion is that one of these test launches came down in the Ivdel area. While this is possible, there is a lack of evidence to back it up in the form of what rockets were involved and exactly where they were being launched from.

Overall, the possibility that a rocket or missile had landed close by is unlikely, as there was no signs of the blast from an explosion or any debris that one would have expected to find if any size of rocket or missile had landed and exploded. Trips within the area in later years (in the Chistop test field) have found debris that appears to be military-type rockets, but after the tragedy nothing was seen or found.

The suggestion that a rocket or missile had landed close by or even some distance away still does not explain the behaviour of the group and why they were found so far from the tent in the circumstances they were found in. Assuming a tremendous explosion occurred within an area close to the tent, why were only three of the group subjected to such massive internal injuries? It can be understood that a loud explosion and flames may have caused them to exit the tent in the manner they did, but the rush to get so far away is incomprehensible, particularly as nothing was found near enough to the tent to make them do this.

Infrasound weapon

The hypothesis of the worst of the injuries being caused by the testing of some type of sound weapon or infrasonic weapon is based more on an attempt to explain how the injuries may have been caused rather than any evidence at Kholat Syakhl or the immediate area that might lead to a conclusion that such a weapon (assuming it existed) was actually used.

The adherents of this theory point to the work of Dr Vladimir Gavreau, who was originally born in Russia but was actually a French scientist. Other than his work on an infrasonic whistle, the link with the Dyatlov group deaths is tenuous to say the least and appears to be based on the fact that he was born in Russia and had a connection with infrasonics. The emphasis on Gavreau appears to be that if he was working on infrasonics with a potential military application then so must the Soviets, although there is absolutely no evidence whatsoever to back this up.[8] From 1948 into the 1960s Gavreau was living and working in France, based in Marseille. He worked on robotics with potential military applications and presented various papers, including one on 16 November 1959 with Albert Calaora on acoustics. During this period in the late 1950s (and into the 1960s), Dr Gavreau also conducted a number of experiments in sound waves. It should be stressed that these experiments were primarily in the acoustic range as opposed to purely infrasonic, as is sometimes implied. During his research, Gavreau discovered that the nausea being experienced by himself and other workers within the building where they carried out their research was due to a large ventilator fan being driven by a low-speed motor that had not been fixed properly to its mountings. The resulting vibrations were giving off a very low frequency sound, which had been affecting them.

Although there is absolutely no correlation between the work that Gavreau carried out in France and what happened to the Dyatlov group 2,500 miles (4,000km) away in the Urals, it is felt that the worst of the internal injuries to Semyon Zolotarev, Luda Dubinina and Rustem Slobodin was possibly caused by a similar weapon being developed by the Soviet military and tested in the northern Urals, either directly or indirectly on members of the Dyatlov group.

The first problem with this theory is the work of Dr Vladimir Gavreau himself: his experiments and theories tend to attract dedicated conspiracy theorists who find in his work what they want to find and ignore anything that may conflict with their theories. A current expert in the field of infrasonics has described Vladimir Gavreau himself as a 'nut job' (this view was directly expressed to the author). Whilst this less than flattering description of Gavreau is somewhat subjective, there is no denying that his work tends to attract dedicated conspiracy theorists. Another of Gavreau's supporters was the author William S. Burroughs, whose writing is described as 'paranoid fiction'.

The second problem with the theory is that although intense infrasound can cause serious damage to a human body (150dB of any sound above 5Hz is harmful to humans), it would not have caused some of the worst injuries found on Semyon Zolotarev, Luda Dubinina and Nicolai Thibeaux-Brignolle. Intense infrasound causes internal damage such as soft tissue damage, ruptured blood vessels, nausea and disorientation. It does not cause internal mechanical damage of the kind found on the three Dyatlov group members, which were broken ribs and fractures.

Last but not least, there is no evidence of a Soviet military infrasonic weapon at this time, although work on something of this nature would have been highly classified in 1959 and would probably remain so today. Another problem with the theory is that even if a weapon of this nature had been available at the time, its size would have made it extremely difficult to transport it with any ease. A current unit today in use at a research facility for infrasonics in the USA, which has an output of 120dB at 5Hz, has the same footprint as a 40ft shipping container. Any unit of this nature potentially used by the Soviet military in February 1959 would be likely to have been as large if not larger. The possibility that it would have been taken by either a tracked vehicle or large wheeled carrier of the type used to carry missiles – or even slung underneath a helicopter and taken into the winter blizzard conditions of the northern Urals for testing – is extremely unlikely.

Mansi legends and murder by Mansi tribesmen

The supposed murder by the Mansi of a female geologist in the area in the 1930s has led some to believe that the Mansi had killed the Dyatlov party as they were enraged by the group's encroachment on two sacred Mansi sites (Kholat Syakhl and Mount Otorten). Another theory suggests that the Mansi may have killed the members of the group in order to get any alcohol they may have had, although Yury Yudin is adamant they had none with them. The story of the murdered female geologist has not been verified by anyone and, even assuming it were true – that the geologist had encroached on sacred Mansi sites such as Mount Otorten or Kholat Syakhl and it was proved that she was murdered for doing so – there is no evidence to suggest that the Mansi had killed any of the members of the Dyatlov group. In the first place, there is the absence of footprints or any signs of a struggle having taken place. Whilst it is possible that guns may have been used to keep the Dyatlov party subdued whilst the Mansi murdered them, the group could possibly have run down the mountain away from someone threatening them. None of the signs at the tent, or the tracks leading towards the tree line, suggest there was anyone else present. It would have taken more than one individual with a gun to be able to threaten the party and then kill all of them. The help given by the Mansi hunters in searching for the missing party appears to have been willingly given, and while it could be said that they assisted the search party in order to deflect attention away from themselves, it appears to be unlikely. Mansi hunters and their dogs found the bodies of Zina Kolmogorova and Rustem Slobodin.

There is a final possibility that had Mansi hunters been involved – and had they been able to cover any tracks they had made – the deaths of Luda Dubinina, Semyon Zolotarev and Nicolai Thibeaux-Brignolle are unexplained. It does not seem possible that the Mansi would have been able to cause these injuries without leaving external marks on the bodies of the victims.

One interesting aside on the involvement of the Mansi is that a family of Mansi who lived close to Mount Otorten said that they had seen someone (possibly members of the Dyatlov group) coming down Mount Otorten at some point after 1 February from a distance of approximately 1–1.5 miles (2–3km). Whether they may have observed another party or were not telling the truth is not known. In any event, their sighting was not taken into account in the official findings.

Murder by escaped prisoners

Although Stalin had been dead for nearly six years by February 1959, the Soviet Union was still a repressive state. Despite the thaw in the USSR after Khrushchev came to power, the Gulags still existed, even though by early 1959 many prisoners had been released. The height of the thaw was in 1960, although the numbers incarcerated started to grow again after Brezhnev came to power.[9] A joke in the Soviet Union was that you could either be inside in one of the camps or outside in the bigger prison (i.e. the USSR).[10] The Gulag system began in 1929 and was used to incarcerate both criminal and political prisoners. The system of camps stretched right across the USSR, with many in the most barren and desolate areas. Although the conditions inside the camps were bad enough, to escape from one of them would have required considerable luck and ingenuity as well as a high degree of hardiness just to stay alive as the conditions outside the camps were so inhospitable, especially in midwinter. There were a number of camps on both sides of the northern Urals that would not have been a great distance from Kholat Syakhl, with the camp system at Ivdel being the closest. The prisoners of the Ivdel camps were put to work in mining, road construction and working in the forests on lumber, so there would have been numerous opportunities for escape attempts to be made. The Dyatlov group had also passed through Ivdel on 25 January 1959 on their way north from Serov to Vizhay prior to starting their journey on foot. Another camp system lay 370 miles (594km) to the north of Kholat Syakhl at Vorkuta, which was as desolate and harsh as any in the system. German PoWs had also laboured there in the coal mines in the immediate post-war years. There had been a revolt by prisoners at Vorkuta in July 1953, which resulted in over fifty deaths when the revolt was put down without mercy. An American, Homer Harold Cox, also spent time in Vorkuta after being kidnapped in East Berlin in September 1949; he died of pneumonia a year after he was released in December

1953. There were also further camps on the western side of the northern Urals in the Komi Republic.

Any escaped prisoners certainly would not have harboured any feelings of goodwill towards anyone they ran into, for the fear of being turned in to the authorities. A recaptured prisoner could expect the harshest of punishments, including, quite possibly, execution.

There were two main groups of prisoners in the camps, ordinary criminals and people incarcerated for political crimes. Oddly, the authorities treated escapes and attempted escapes by the political prisoners far more seriously than they did the ordinary criminals. An escape by a political prisoner would involve a search party being formed immediately, possibly involving frontier guards. Additionally, nearby towns and settlements would be warned to be on the lookout for them.[11]

It may be doubted that escaped criminals would use extreme violence or murder during their escape bids after they had left the vicinity of a camp, but their desperation can perhaps be illustrated by an example. With many of the camps being in remote areas, one of the biggest problems for anyone escaping and making their way to some form of civilisation was the problem of sustenance on the journey. A known practice – one that was common enough to have its own nickname – was for a potential escapee to identify someone who would make the escape with him (or her) on the basis that the two of them would stand a better chance of succeeding. Once they had escaped and hunger started to become a problem, the person who had initiated the escape would kill his or her companion and eat them. This applied to larger groups of escapees as well, where unfortunate victims would be identified beforehand and set upon when the time was right. The nickname for these victims was 'Walking Larders'.[12]

In respect of the Dyatlov group, it is highly improbable that they were killed by escaped prisoners. There are a number of reasons: there were no other footprints in the snow either in the vicinity of the tent or around the bodies of the group or in the vicinity; there were nine members in the Dyatlov group, all of whom were fit and strong and, in the absence of weapons, it would have taken a substantial group of escaped prisoners to either kill or overpower them; although escaped prisoners would try to stay hidden as much as possible, criminals who would be more likely to use extreme violence tended to head for towns and cities where they would have a support network (including false documentation) from other criminals and blend into the surroundings. Political prisoners would do their best to try and get out of the Soviet Union if they could,[12] as they were more reviled than other criminals. Any attempt by political prisoners to make contact with people they had formerly known brought these people into as great a danger as the political prisoners themselves, as they would almost certainly meet the same fate from the authorities if they were found to be harbouring or helping them. Finally, there appears to be no reason why the Dyatlov group would have been attacked by escaped prisoners. They were in their tent getting ready to bed down for the night, so would not have observed anyone who may not have wanted their presence reported to the authorities. Neither was anything removed from the tent that may have proved to be of use to someone on the run, such as ski equipment, torches, knives or footwear.

Special forces

As with a number of the other theories, there is more than one sub-theory involved regarding the group meeting their deaths at the hands of special forces troops (see also Chapter 7, Political theory). This main theory rests on the premise that the group were all killed by special forces troops for the reason that they could not be allowed to live after seeing them (the troops themselves in the case of Americans) or had witnessed secret tests (in the case of Soviet troops).

The injuries received by some of the Dyatlov group did point to a fight of some kind and this fight may have involved special forces troops. The hand injuries sustained by Igor Dyatlov and Rustem Slobodin suggest a fight of some kind. Also, the grey foamy discharge that was found on the cheek of Yury Doroshenko led some doctors to believe that something or someone had been pressing on his chest cavity.

American special forces

The use of US special forces in this region in the 1950s may not be quite as fanciful as it first seems. When concerns arose over the 'Bomber Gap' (see Chapter 2) in 1954–55, there was deep concern in the USA over the size and capabilities of the Soviet Union's strategic bomber forces. Although high-altitude balloons with a photographic reconnaissance capability were briefly used by the US Air Force (under the codename Project Genetrix) in early 1956, they were nowhere near satisfactory. The first U-2 spy flights over the Eastern bloc and the Soviet Union started later in 1956. However, there was a desperate and insatiable requirement for more accurate intelligence. The paranoia and extremely tight security in the Soviet Union made the insertion of external civilian spies extremely difficult and the proposal was examined of sending in US special forces to gather intelligence on the airfields where the Soviet bombers were based. In the event, the idea was not proceeded with, as it was viewed as impractical and eventually the 'Bomber Gap' was proved by 1956–57 to be a completely false notion, with the evidence for this provided by the U-2 overflights of the USSR. The U-2 overflights, however, could not cover everything of interest.

There were no Soviet long-range bomber bases on either side of the Urals where the Dyatlov incident took place. However, by 1959 the USSR had constructed a number of Arctic airbases, with the majority close to the Soviet Arctic coastline. These were known as 'Bounce Aerodromes' as they were intended to allow Soviet bombers attacking the USA to land and top up with fuel before making their journey over the Polar icecap. The nearest 'Bounce Aerodrome' would have been at Vorkuta 370 miles (594km) north of where the Dyatlov group were located; the area around Kholat Syakhl is unlikely to be a place where any American or Western forces would place themselves to keep an eye on what was happening at Vorkuta. However, one place that would have been of great interest to such forces was the facility at Nizhnyaya Tura for the production and storage of nuclear weapons. This facility would have been passed on the way north by the Dyatlov group and was within a reasonable distance for a group of special forces to make their way to from Kholat Syakhl. In 1958–59 the CIA was only just finding out what was going on there, as they knew that there was a facility in the area consuming a large amount of power, in addition to the gas diffusion plant further south at Verkh Neyvinsk, near Serov, which was enriching plutonium U-235.

Without any further evidence, however, the balance of probability is that US or Western forces are unlikely to have been involved in the Dyatlov group deaths.

Soviet special forces (Spetznatz)
The suggestion for the involvement of Soviet special forces is that the Dyatlov group had stumbled across and witnessed the testing of secret weapons and needed to be eliminated to

ensure their silence. This is an extremely remote possibility. Despite the presence of possible military testing areas, (including the Chistop massif) in the vicinity of where the group was located, the testing appears to have been of a conventional nature. Additionally, numerous groups made trips into these mountains, along with the Mansi who traversed the area herding reindeer and hunting. It would seem an odd choice for a place to test weapons in conditions of the utmost secrecy. Also, the hypothermia deaths and the massive internal injuries received by Luda Dubinina, Semyon Zolotarev and Nicolai Thibeaux-Brignolle do not appear to be the type of injuries they would have received from these troops. Also, if the requirement had been to eliminate the group completely, then it would be expected that their bodies would have been better concealed rather than just left to be covered by snow.

One much less plausible theory, and a very shaky one at that, which attempts to explain the lack of footprints around the area of the tent and tree line, is that a helicopter hovered close to the tent and ordered members of the group to get in. Possibly part of the group were told to get into the helicopter while the others ran for safety to the tree line. After interrogation, these first three were pushed out of the helicopter into the snow while the helicopter went after the rest of the group at the edge of the forest. Both Krivonischenko and Doroshenko died of hypothermia after trying to build a fire. Kolevatov may have run into the ravine to try and build a good shelter but did not succeed and died. The remaining members of the group (Zolotarev, Dubinina and Thibeaux-Brignolle) were possibly picked up by the helicopter and interrogated. They were then dropped to their deaths from a height, which would explain the massive internal injuries they received , although there were no external marks to account for them.

Whilst this scenario is a physical possibility and explains the lack of other footprints besides the group's footprints, it fails to explain any reason or motive as to why a military helicopter should pick up members of the Dyatlov group and interrogate them before throwing them to their deaths. It is possible that there was something that the military did not want anyone to see, but even given a state as brutal as the Soviet Union could be at that time, it still seems far-fetched that a party of reasonably well-connected university students should all be murdered to ensure their silence. The group were known to be in the area and were making their trip in honour of the 21st Communist Party Congress in Moscow, so any serious mistreatment of them would be bound to draw attention.

Against these arguments of murder by Soviet special forces, however, is the political theory outlined in Chapter 7.

Flashfire within the tent

One theory as to why they left the tent in such a panic is that the stove they were using for cooking caused some kind of a flashfire, which shot right through the tent and alarmed everyone so much that they slashed their way out of the side of the tent, as the stove may have been in the way of their exiting from the front.

Although a flashfire may have been a shock to everyone inside the tent and in their panic they slashed their way out, it would not be expected for the group to have gone so far away from the tent (initially nearly 1 mile (1.6km)), especially in deep snow that would have made the going hard for them. Flashfires are literally just that: over in a flash.

However, the most significant piece of evidence with regard to this theory is that the home-made stove, which was built by Igor Dyatlov, was found to be in the stowed position when the tent was discovered by the search parties.

Having said this, the group were estimated to have had their meal not long before they exited the tent, so possibly something in the nature of a flashfire may actually have occurred. Despite the appalling way that the search parties gathered everything up into a jumble, with no attempt to preserve the initial scene as they had found it, there was no mention by anybody or in any part of the written investigation of the appearance of burn or scorch marks on the tent.

Neither does the behaviour of the group after they left the tent support the theory of a flashfire. After having gone down to the tree line, they appeared to have stayed there for some time. It was deduced that at least Krivonischenko and Doroshenko (the first two bodies found) had been climbing the cedar tree to break branches off to burn, but it is also believed that they may have been looking at the tent from the higher part of the cedar tree. By the time they had reached the tree line, any fire would have been long over at the tent and it would have been expected that they would immediately try to make their way back. Whatever had scared them enough to run away from the tent, and stay away from it, must have been far worse than a flashfire.

A variation on the flashfire inside the tent is that, possibly, once the evening meal had been finished and the group settled down to sleep, at some point the stove may have become blocked, and thick choking smoke may have filled the tent rapidly, causing them to slash at the sides of the tent to be able to breathe and also let the smoke escape. Once the group were outside the tent an argument may have broken out as to who was responsible for the blockage being caused, which may have developed into a physical fight with the group splitting into two camps. This would help to explain why the two parties were separate from each other when the search parties discovered the bodies. It does not explain though, as with the flashfire theory, why they were so far from the tent and why they stayed away so long, with a minimum of clothing and footwear. Finally, notwithstanding the burn injuries (caused by the fire at the cedar tree to Doroschenko and Krivonischenko, none of the other injuries are those which would be as a result of a flashfire.

Radiation and KGB theory

One of the oddest facets of the whole investigation is the presence of radiation on the bodies and some clothes. A theory has been put forward by Alexey Rakitin to explain the presence of radiation. He believes that Semyon Zolotarev, Alexander Kolevatov and George Krivonischenko were undercover KGB agents who, acting as ski tourists, were to meet with foreign intelligence agents on the route they were taking. These foreign agents were also to appear under the cover of another tourist group and, once they met up, they were to perform a 'controlled transfer' of radioactive clothes (a transfer of fake samples of radioactive materials in the form of items of clothing contaminated with radioactive dust that was intended to mislead the foreign agents). Rakitin believes that the spies somehow discovered the group's connections to the KGB, or possibly the 'outsider' group made a mistake themselves (gave themselves away by wrong use of a Russian idiom, lack of knowledge of a fact in common knowledge in the USSR, etc). The foreign agents decided to eliminate the evidence and made the tourists undress and leave the tent, using the threat of firearms but without shooting them, so that their deaths would look natural from cold. Rustem Slobodin tried to resist the attackers, he was beaten hard but could walk. As the group was moving away from the tent, he lost consciousness. His absence was noticed after some time and Igor Dyatlov went to look for Slobodin. After he too failed to return, Zina Kolmogorova went to search for them. Eventually all three died of hypothermia. A fire was lit by the surviving members of the group so that the others could find their way back more easily. The foreign agents near the tent saw the fire and that the tourists had somehow managed to organise themselves enough to survive, and it was decided to kill them. By that time the survivors had dispersed, and, as each one was found, the agents used torture and close combat methods to get them to admit to their KGB involvement. They were then liquidated. This accounted for the serious injuries, the missing tongue of Luda Dubinina and the missing eyeballs of others. Also this use of violence would account for the grey foam discharge from Yury Doroshenko's mouth being caused by something or someone pressing on his chest cavity.

The bodies of the four tourists discovered later in May had been pushed down into the gully in order to make their discovery difficult. The spies searched the tent and the dead bodies and took away any cameras that may have been used to photograph them (the spies) but left others. They also took the tourists' notes made before their deaths. A slight variation on this theory is that when Krivonischenko was arrested by the police for singing at Serov railway station, this was just a ruse for the KGB to pass the radioactive contaminated clothes to him for the transfer to the foreign agents later on in the mountains. Krivonischenko, of course, had a link to nuclear materials when he worked at the closed city, Chelyabinsk-40, and was involved in the clean-up after the nuclear accident there.

It is also considered odd by most observers that Lev Ivanov, the chief investigator, used a Geiger counter at the scene, as no explanation was given for its use. Another possible explanation for the presence of radiation in the bodies and on some clothes is that the group used a thorium gas mantle lamp. thorium is radioactive and produces a radioactive gas, Radon-220, as one of its decay products. Particles from the 'fallout' of a thorium gas mantle lamp occur over a period of time and can be inhaled as well as ingested with food or drink. However, a 1981 study found that by using a gas thorium mantle every weekend for a year a person would be exposed to approximately 0.3–0.6mrem, which is a tiny amount.

Fight amongst Dyatlov group

Another theory that may have some credence is the possibility of a fight breaking out between two or more of the party. The autopsies showed that Igor Dyatlov and Rustem Slobodin had hand injuries that are common in fights using fists. The possibility is that a fight had broken out in the tent and spilled outside, but it does not adequately explain why the tent was slashed and – had knives been available – why they were not used in the fight. It seems strange that knives would have been used to slash a way out of the tent but then been discarded. Another variation is that a furious argument had broken out within the tent and that the slashing had been done in a fury, with the antagonists going some distance away from the tent to settle their dispute. Equally, another possible variation is that the argument had broken out within the tent with the whole group getting involved and separating into two factions, with possibly George Krivonischenko and Yury Doroshenko leaving the tent in a fury and saying they would make their own camp at the tree line. Realising the folly of this, by going out into the extreme cold without adequate protection, the others may have gone to find them, then almost immediately become lost and disoriented, eventually all of them succumbing to the extreme conditions.

There were two known possibilities of the potential to cause a fight. The first was the male attention towards Zina

Kolmogorova. The three males who were involved were Igor Dyatlov, Yury Doroshenko and Semyon Zolotarev. Igor Dyatlov was considered to be her current love interest at the time. At some point on the evening of 1 February, while they were getting ready to bed down for the night, possibly either Zolotarev or Doroshenko may have made some kind of pass at Zina Kolmogorova which enraged Dyatlov and started an immediate fight. As has already been mentioned, Zolotarev had fought in the military during the Second World War and, in addition, his record book from the Minsk Institute of Physical Education showed that he had been trained in unarmed combat, so he would have been quite capable of using physical force if the occasion arose.

The second possibility to have the potential to cause a fight was the antagonism displayed by George Krivonischenko, who had an explosive temper. After being asked to sleep by the stove, his outburst on the night of 28/29 January would certainly have caused at least some members of the group to be wary of him. The tone and demeanour of the group was subdued on the day following his outburst, showing that his behaviour had some effect.

Whilst there is a certain plausibility to these possibilities, it seems hard to believe that the remaining members of the group would have ventured into the darkness without adequate protection and without due care and attention to where they were going so that they could find their way back to the safety of the tent. By this point the tent had been badly damaged but it was not beyond their capabilities to cover the damage. Equally, the shock of having a serious fight break out, along with the serious damage to their dwelling, may have made them far less rational and less aware to the danger they were all in by exposing themselves to the elements in the manner they did. It does go some way, however, to explaining why there were two groups apart from each other with perhaps one group favouring Zina Kolmogorova and Igor Dyatlov, and the other group favouring the rival, who may have been Zolotarev. Yet this scenario does not account for the massive internal injuries suffered by Luda Dubinina, Semyon Zolotarev and Nicolai Thibeaux-Brignolle. In addition to the injuries on these three, it is believed that someone or something had been pressing on the chest cavity of Yury Doroshenko. The question also has to be asked would Luda Dubinina have been attacked so violently in a fight between males over another female?

It was said that alcohol had been present in the tent. This is totally denied by Yury Yudin, the surviving member of the group, who says that they had no alcohol. He knows this as, being the group medic, he had wanted some for medical purposes early on in the trip. He also mentioned to Zina Kolmogorova when he left that there was no alcohol, as she took over his position as group medic when he turned back. Yury Yudin did say in 2012 that there was a possibility that Krivonischenko may have had a canister of alcohol in his backpack; he would have been better placed to get it from contacts in the closed city where he had worked as it was more readily available there. Yudin was only referring to ethyl alcohol, not vodka. Ethyl alcohol was very difficult to get hold of at the time but, as he said, it may have been in Krivonischenko's backpack. Yet there is no evidence to suggest that any alcohol was consumed, or consumed in such a quantity to have either caused a fight to break out or cause members of the group to throw caution to the wind and make their way out of the tent completely unprepared for the elements.

Wild animals
The greatest threat to the group from wild animals would have come from bears and packs of wolves. There are

different groups of Russian bears, with some closely related to North American bears, some being the same size as their grizzly cousins in the USA. The most widespread form of brown bear in Eurasia is the 'common' brown bear (*ursus arctos arctos*); these bears are regularly encountered in the northern Urals. For the most part they tend to avoid hikers and other humans in the remote Taiga and mountains. They are nevertheless dangerous and on average ten people a year in Russia are killed by them. Bears hibernate in winter from around early autumn to early spring, although they do not hibernate as deeply as other animals and can be woken up.[13] Bears that awaken early from hibernation are highly aggressive and dangerous. In most of western, central and southern Siberia, these bears are heavily dependent on Siberian pine (cedar) for their main food source. If this food source fails in any way, bears start killing livestock and attacking people – and do not hibernate when they are in this state. They continue looking for food in the deep snow until they starve to death or kill something to eat. Any unarmed hikers running into a bear at this time would run a high risk of being attacked and killed. These bears are known as '*shatun*' (wanderer) and are responsible for the majority of human fatalities. In periods when there is not enough food for bears, they have been known to raid graveyards for corpses to eat.

At the time of the deaths of the Dyatlov group, it is a virtual certainty that bears in the area would have still been hibernating. Also, there were no tracks of a bear either by the tent, by the footprints of the group or near where the bodies were found. The slashes on the tent fabric were made by members of the group using knives to escape from inside the tent rather than anything slashing from the outside. None of any of the injuries on any of the members of the group had been caused by a bear.

While it is fairly certain that bears would have been hibernating in January and February, wolves do not hibernate and in January/February they would have been hungry and looking for food in any shape or form they could find it. Their usual diet is rabbit, but when their food supply becomes scarce, packs of wolves are known to widen their search for food and start encroaching on areas where livestock are kept. Wolves tend to hunt in packs of six or seven. A large pack could number thirty to forty and, if they were hungry enough, would not be deterred by even a large group of unarmed hikers. Wolves will start to attack more dangerous prey when they run out of non-dangerous prey. In February 2011, a 'superpack' of over 400 wolves were responsible for killing large numbers of horses at Verkhoyansk in Siberia (although the size of this 'superpack' has been disputed as being a ridiculous number).[14] There were twenty-four separate teams of hunters assembled to deal with them.

But once again, as with the possibility of an attack by a bear, the slashes to the fabric on the tent were not made by a wild animal and there was nothing at all in the area to indicate in the form of tracks, the presence of wolves. Also, none of the injuries suffered by the group were consistent with an attack by a pack of wolves, or indeed any type of animal.

UFOs/light spheres

Invariably, whenever a case involving strange deaths or disappearances in the open or wild is discussed, the question of unidentified flying objects and extraterrestrials arises. One item in particular is the mention of lights or light spheres in the night skies. One aspect of these lights is examined in much greater detail in Chapter 8 (the Yury Yakimov theory).

This unusual phenomenon of light spheres was observed in the skies in 1959 (and also later) in different parts of the northern Urals and also in Ivdel. The movement of light spheres across the sky, their shape and time of appearance are described similarly by Mansi hunters, tourists (i.e. hikers/skiers), meteorologists, the military and occasional observers. There are three possible explanations for these lights: they were tests of missiles, they were UFOs (or alien craft), or they were afterburners from Soviet fighter aircraft. Theorists in connection with the Dyatlov incident have focused on the presence of large lights in the night sky on 1 February. These lights were described as bright orbs and were seen by another group of ski hikers/tourists about 30 miles (48km) south of the Dyatlov group's location. The UFO theorists claim the brightly lit orbs were responsible in some way for what happened to the Dyatlov group. Yet there is nothing to support the theory other than the fact that some members of the group suffered massive injuries that appeared to have no immediate rational explanation. There were no unexplained tracks or traces around the tent, along the route the party took, or around the areas where the bodies were found to suggest there was anyone or anything else there.

One further item that the UFO theorists have alighted on is the last photograph in one of the cameras that was found in the tent by the search parties. When it was developed, this photograph appeared to have been overexposed and showed what appeared to be bright lights against a black background, which gives some credence to the UFO theory, or at least to the theory that the bright orbs that had been observed in the sky had something to do with what happened to the group. However, it is also possible that the photo was genuinely an overexposure. It has also been suggested that the overexposure of that particular photo was caused by a member of the search party, who may have picked up the camera and accidentally caused the camera to take a picture that was badly exposed.

If the orbs had come close to the tent, one would have expected the members of the group to observe them in puzzlement at first, as presumably no noise was made by them. The evacuation of the tent in a complete panic does not support this view and, if a picture had been taken of the orbs, it would seem to suggest that whoever took the picture had left the camera behind whilst running for his or her life. Whatever had happened strongly suggests that it happened in a matter of seconds and caused them to immediately tear their way out of the tent, which does not create a scenario for taking photographs.

Other than the sightings of lights in the sky, much of which has immediate rational explanations, there is no other evidence to support the UFO theory, other than possibly the sheer strangeness of the deaths and where the bodies were found.

According to data collected by the International Ufologist Union, in the first eleven months of 2005 there were 2,348 sightings of worldwide UFOs (reported in the newspaper *Komsomolskaya Pravda* dated 9 December 2005).

One most unexpected supporter of UFOs being involved in the deaths of the Dyatlov group was Lev Ivanov, the lead criminal investigator on the case. However, other than the appearance of lights/fire spheres/glowing orbs in the night skies of the northern Ural Mountains there is no other firm evidence to back up the theory, other than possibly the serious internal injuries to Luda Dubinina, Semyon Zolotarev and Nicolai Thibeaux-Brignolle, which appear to be almost inexplicable.

Yeti/Siberian trolls

In early November 2012 it was reported in the media that Professor Valentin Sapunov of the Russian State Hydrometeorological University claimed to have found hair in a remote Siberian cave a year previously, possibly belonging to a human-like mammal unknown to man. He had estimated that there were up to 200 yeti living in the Altai, Kemerovo and Khakassia regions of Siberia and explained that none had been sighted as they had an acute sense of danger. Sapunov's claims regarding the hair were played down by Oleg Pugachev, Director of the Zoological Institute of the Russian Academy of Science. Pugachev said that it was impossible to verify the DNA due to a lack of hair bulbs, and stated that the structure of the hair showed it could have belonged to a goat, bear or other animal. Nevertheless, there is strong interest in the possibility of a yeti or similar type of creature being found.

One theory is that the members of the group all fell victim to some form of malign Siberian troll or group of trolls, or possibly a yeti-type creature. Whilst no one has ever produced concrete evidence of the existence of these trolls or yetis, what the theorists of the Dyatlov incident have focused on is a comment in the *Evening Otorten*, the 'joke newspaper' made by the group: 'We now know that Snowmen exist.' There is no other reference in the diaries to this statement and neither is the statement expanded upon. As already stated (in Chapter 5), there is some dispute about the dates of the *Evening Otorten* and also whether the comment about the 'Snowmen' is actually true, but with the paper having disappeared, nothing can be verified. Once again, a different meaning is ascribed to the last photograph taken by the group (see UFOs/light spheres, above), which appears to show lights. This picture, actually from Igor Dyatlov's camera, is taken by some of the troll/ yeti theorists to show a pair of hands grabbing forward. The whole theory – which also attempts to account for the worst of the internal injuries by the fact of a powerful creature squeezing the victims without leaving external marks – is very flimsy. There is virtually nothing to substantiate it and, again, we come back to the issue of a lack of footprints, as it would be assumed that these trolls or yetis would at least make some form of track.

The lair of the golden woman[15]

The leading researchers in this field (the paranormal) in relation to the USSR are Paul Stonehill and Philip Mantle. They have researched this subject for many years and, at the time of writing, they are currently working on a project to explain the events concerning the deaths of the Dyatlov group, which involves the 'golden woman' (in Russian *zolotaya baba*). They hope to publish the results of their research very shortly. The 'golden woman' is a well-known phenomenon in the northern Urals and has a long history, believed to stem from the Khanty and Mansi ancestors' (Ob-Ugric people) contact with ancient peoples in the north of India, or possibly Sumerians in Southern Mesopotamia. The lair of the 'golden woman' is believed to lie close to Mount Otorten and, throughout its history, the lair was closely guarded by the ancestors of the present-day Khanti and Mansi people. The actual deaths of the Dyatlov group, who may have come close to the lair of the 'golden woman', are believed to have been caused by a form of directed energy. Little comment can be made until Paul Stonehill and Philip Mantle publish the results of their investigations.

ДОРОШЕНКО Ю А. ДУБИНИНА Л А. ДЯТЛОВ И А.

ЗОЛАТАРЕВ А И КОЛМОГОРОВА З А КОЛЕВАТОВ А С

КРИВОНИШЕНКО Г А СЛОБОДИН Р В ТИБО-БРИНЬОЛЬ Н В

1 The memorial by the graves in Mikhailovskoe Cemetery. *Author*

2 Memorial plaque on a rock at Dyatlov Pass. *Courtesy Dyatlov Memorial Foundation*

3 Eight of the ten members of the Dyatlov group (Doroshenko and Krivonischenko are missing). They are all well wrapped up against the wind and cold and seemingly all in good spirits. The GAZ-63 truck eventually left Vizhay at 1.10 p.m. on 26 January 1959. *Courtesy Dyatlov Memorial Foundation*

4 At the woodcutters' settlement, 41st Kvartal. Igor Dyatlov is second from left. Luda is fourth from left and Zina is seated on the steps. *Courtesy Dyatlov Memorial Foundation*

5 28 January 1959, abandoned geologists' settlement – Yury Yudin decides to turn back, a decision that saves his life. Before he leaves, he is being hugged by Luda who was very fond of him. Igor Dyatlov (left) and Nicolai Thibeaux-Brignolle (right) look on. *Courtesy Dyatlov Memorial Foundation*

6 The Dyatlov group's tent with the chimney from the stove at the front. The stove had been built by Igor Dyatlov. *Courtesy Dyatlov Memorial Foundation*

7 L to R: Dubinina, Slobodin, Zolotarev, Thibeaux-Brignolle. At this point the going was not too hard. The ground was to get steeper and the snow was to increase in depth. *Courtesy Dyatlov Memorial Foundation*

8 L to R: Nicolai Thibeaux-Brignolle, Luda Dubinina, Semyon Zolotarev and Zina Kolmogorova. *Courtesy Dyatlov Memorial Foundation*

9 Zina Kolmogorova on skis. Luda Dubinina is standing at the rear. *Courtesy Dyatlov Memorial Foundation*

10 Taking a break. Although well wrapped up against the elements, the conditions in this photo are not as extreme as the group would meet only a short time later. *Courtesy Dyatlov Memorial Foundation*

11 L to R: Luda Dubinina and Yury Doroshenko pose (left) while Nicolai Thibeaux-Brignolle and Rustem Slobodin fool around (right). *Courtesy Dyatlov Memorial Foundation*

12 1 February 1959, the penultimate photograph of the Dyatlov group. Here they are making their way up on to the ridge on Kholat Syakhl where they were to pitch the tent on their last night. The weather has worsened considerably. *Courtesy Dyatlov Memorial Foundation*

13 The last photograph taken of the Dyatlov group while they were still alive. Here they are preparing to pitch their tent on Kholat Syakhl in the late afternoon of 1 February 1959. Sometime that evening or night, something caused them to slash their way out of the tent and down the mountain with no footwear and minimal clothing. *Courtesy Dyatlov Memorial Foundation*

14 26 February 1959 – the tent is found. The small wooden cross on the far side of the tent can be seen in the foreground of the picture taken of the Dyatlov group while they are preparing to pitch the tent on 1 February. Boris Slobtsov (left), Yury Koptelov (squatting on right). *Courtesy Dyatlov Memorial Foundation*

15 Footprints found close to the tent. *Courtesy Dyatlov Memorial Foundation*

16 One of the search party stands in a den that the Dyatlov group had tried to build in order to protect themselves from the cold and wind. The bodies of Luda Dubinina, Nicolai Thibeaux-Brignolle, Semyon Zolotarev and Alexander Kolevatov were found in this area. *Courtesy Dyatlov Memorial Foundation*

17 The cedar tree that members of the Dyatlov group had climbed and broken branches from for the fire. The bodies of George Krivonischenko and Yury Doroshenko were found close to this tree with the remains of a fire. *Courtesy Dyatlov Memorial Foundation*

18 One of the bodies is moved. *Courtesy Dyatlov Memorial Foundation*

19 Another view of one of the bodies being removed. *Courtesy Dyatlov Memorial Foundation*

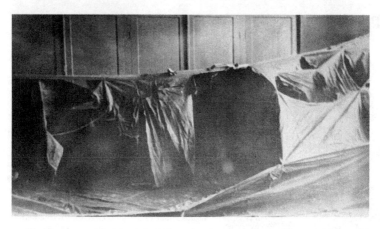

20 The tent re-erected to show the slash marks. No one appears to know what happened to the tent after the investigation was over. *Courtesy Dyatlov Memorial Foundation*

21 The Antonov An-2 used in the search operation operated from the airfield at Ivdel. *Courtesy Dyatlov Memorial Foundation*

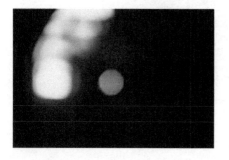

22 The last photo taken on Igor Dyatlov's camera is a source of much speculation. Some take this as proof of the light orbs, others say someone's face can be seen in it. More mundanely, it has been said that when one of the search party lifted the camera from the tent, they pressed the button and took a picture by mistake (with the lens cap partially on) and this is the result. No one knows for certain. *Courtesy Dyatlov Memorial Foundation*

7

What happened – alternative locations

All of the previous theories mentioned in Chapter 6 are concerned with the events taking place on the eastern slopes of Kholat Syakhl, i.e. where the abandoned tent was found. There is another line of theories that explain the events having taken place in a completely different location – and that the bodies and all their belongings, including tent and equipment, were brought from another location and transported to Kholat Syakhl.

This theory of outside interference starts to manifest itself in a number of ways when looking at items arising from the investigation. There were a number of inconsistencies. One of the most important is a telegram from Terebilov, Assistant General Prosecutor of the USSR in Moscow, sent on 9 May 1959 to Chief Prosecutor Klinov in Sverdlovsk. Terebilov tells Klinov to send him 'Case No 3/2518-59 related to deaths of student group'. The case file that is generally referred to for public consumption was never given a case number and this suggests that there is another file held by the authorities. There is one other reference to Case No 3/2518-59 in a letter dated 16 May 1959. Requests to see this file have been refused by the chief prosecutor of the Oblast and there is no explanation as to why the file in the public domain does not have a case number.

There were other inconsistencies. For instance, Yury Yudin had mentioned both he and Zina Kolmogorova had complained that, as acting medics for the group, they did not have any alcohol to use for sterilising. However, one of the items mentioned and itemised on a list as being removed from the tent after it was found was alcohol. Yury Yudin was adamant to his death that they did not take any alcohol with them nor did they obtain any en route. However, Yudin himself assisted in the sorting of the effects from the tent and he recalls holding a flask in each hand which he did not recognise. He says that one was reclaimed by Krivonischenko's family. The base camp storage (for excess items), which was established by the group before they continued up the mountain, was also a source of controversy as Yury Yudin says there were items found there that were not taken by the group.

A number of people associated with the case felt uneasy about the way the whole investigation was conducted, not least by the fact that they had to sign non-disclosure agreements. An example of this uneasiness was the case of a pilot of a Yak-12 light aircraft who flew over the northern Urals looking for forest fires and was involved in the search for the group. He had instructed his wife to take good care of their child in case anything happened to him. He died not long after he had made the comment, and whilst it may have been coincidence, it seemed to fit an outsider's view that something was not right.

There were also clumsy attempts at obscuring a number of details and the group diary shows alterations and amendments as well as items rubbed out. An investigator, Vladimir Korotayev, worked with Investigator Tempalov on the case. Korotayev stated in an interview years later (on 1 February 2008) that he had found a number of inconsistencies in the case but was instructed by his superiors to keep his opinions to himself. Korotayev died on 11 July 2012.

Two physical inconsistencies concerned the tent itself. Some theorists believe that the Dyatlov tent was re-erected wrongly with skis providing support for rope at the ends of the tent instead of at the sides. They have also said that the outlet for the stove was built towards the prevailing wind whereas the tent should have been erected the other way around so that the smoke and any cinders would have been carried away from the tent.

The line of thinking of an alternative location where the deaths occurred has a few sub-theories as to how the group died, but it is all built on the same premise that the authorities were either directly or indirectly involved in the deaths. The thinking goes that once the authorities had either caused the deaths or discovered the deaths, an immediate attempt was made to cover the tracks (literally and figuratively) due to embarrassment. It may be wondered why the authorities would go to so much trouble to falsify the scene and the events relating to the deaths, but once again it must be remembered that the USSR in 1959 was a place where bad news was never welcome. The price for making serious mistakes was much higher than it was in the West. Guilt by association would be enough to earn the wrath of the authorities and could involve imprisonment and loss of privileges such as the flat or house you and your family lived in, with the worst scenario being possible imprisonment or banished to a town in the middle of nowhere. Even as late as the 1970s, crashes of commercial passenger aircraft were rarely publicly reported in Russia; a story was reported in the West of the parents of a young woman who had reported their daughter as missing, only to find on investigation that she had died some time before in a commercial airliner crash belonging to the state airline Aeroflot while on a scheduled flight to Moscow. People in the USSR would generally learn of serious crashes by listening to the BBC or the *Voice of America* radio broadcasts (both of which were officially forbidden).

The 'orderly' descent from the tent does not tie up with the panic stricken attempt to flee from inside it. If this scenario is to be believed, it stretches credulity. The group slashed their way out of the tent in a great hurry then formed an orderly file to walk down the mountain with virtually nothing on their feet and hardly wearing enough clothes to keep themselves warm inside the tent, let alone outside in the deep snow with winds and temperatures of -26°C, before then splitting into what appears to be two different groups.

Before considering the alternative location theory, there is one important item that lends some support to this line of thought, which is that a number of enquirers wondered what the group was doing on the slopes of Kholat Syakhl as it was off the route they were taking to their intended destination of Mount Otorten, which lay 9 miles (15km) to the north of where the tent was found. Following on from the theories concerning possible military involvement (in Chapter 6), one of the main lines of enquiry is that of a military accident and subsequent cover-up by the authorities. There are a number of pieces of evidence to support this view. The files relating to the Dyatlov incident were held by the Russian State Prosecutor's Office for twenty-five years before being transferred to the State Archive and were not available for public viewing (although it must be said that right up to the fall of the Berlin Wall anyone, especially a member of the public, who expressed a desire to go digging through any files held in the Russian State Prosecutor's Office would not only have not got very far, but could well have ended up arrested and imprisoned). One website regarding the Dyatlov tragedy states that the files were not closed and gives the impression that there was no problem for anyone to view them. This appears to have been written by someone who has no knowledge of what was involved in gaining access to potentially contentious files held by either the police or military during the Soviet era.

Once the files became available after the fall of communism, one of the most glaring inconsistencies was on the front of the case file itself. The criminal investigation had been opened on 6 February 1959, which was less than a week after the deaths had taken place but also almost a full week before the time that Igor Dyatlov or another member of the group had intended to send a message from Vizhay to Ural Polytechnic Institute to say they had completed their journey and were returning. To reiterate this very important point: the opening date of the criminal investigation was almost a full week before the group was meant to let everyone know they were okay and on their way home to Sverdlovsk – the telegram was not due to be received at UPI until 12 February 1959. So, in other words, the authorities had started to investigate their deaths before anyone (that is, anyone outside the state authorities, i.e. relatives and the public) knew or had been informed that they were missing or that something was wrong. The file itself basically follows the standard line that the group had slashed their way out of the tent and made their way down to the tree line where they perished.

Notwithstanding the difficulties of gaining access to the files in Soviet times and the numerous anomalies within them, and in view of the apparent attempt to try and obscure the facts, an alternative theory has been developed to explain this. This theory follows the line that the group did not die at the pass at Kholat Syakhl but died elsewhere, and their bodies, along with the tent and their equipment, were brought to Kholat Syakhl in order to give the impression that whatever had happened had taken place at the pass on the slopes of Kholat Syakhl. It should be mentioned here that the tent was wrongly assumed by many to have a standard zipper (as tents do today), but it was actually closed with buttons that were fairly stiff in the stitched canvas; once the front of the tent was buttoned up, there was an inner curtain hung over it for insulation. Under this alternative theory, the slashes were made by a third party to make it look as if the group had tried to get away from the tent in a hurry on the slopes of Kholat Syakhl.

Tu-95M 'Bear' bombers

To start with, the alternative theory of the deaths taking place elsewhere suggests that the route taken by the group was actually to the north of the River Auspia along the River Lozva, which not only makes more sense as it is easier, but this was confirmed by the remaining survivor of the group, Yury Yudin. It will be remembered that Yury Yudin had been taken ill and returned to Sverdlovsk from the second severny, and although he had not gone as far as either the River Auspia or River Lozva with the rest of the group, he nevertheless stated that it was their intention to approach Mount Otorten along the Lozva to the north of the Auspia. While the change in the description of the route may not seem overly significant, slightly to the north of the Lozva was a military testing area. While the Dyatlov group may not have gone into the military test area, they would have been close enough to it in the event of any testing going wrong. Independent testimony was given to a third party from a member of one of the crews of a Soviet bomber. On 1 February 1959, two Tu-95M 'Bear' long-range bombers took off from their base at Uzin, south of Kiev, and headed 1,380 miles (2,220km) north-east to the testing area in the northern Urals. The Tupolev Tu-95M ('Bear' is the NATO codename for the aircraft) first flew in November

1952 and started entering service in 1956 as a long-range strategic nuclear bomber intended to be able to attack the USA. It played a very important role prior to the development of ICBMs and the establishment of submarine-launched ICBMs. The Tu-95M was also intended to be used in a conventional bombing role as well as the nuclear attack role. In 1959 Uzin Airbase was the site for the 106th Heavy Bomber Division (106 TBAD), which comprised two heavy bomber regiments of Tu-95Ms. These were the 409th and 1006th Heavy Bomber Regiments (409 TBAP and 1006 TBAP). The two aircraft that took off from Uzin Airbase on 1 February 1959 were testing air mines, which were dropped by parachute and set to explode above the ground at various heights. During the Second World War, these air mines had been used by both the Luftwaffe and the RAF to devastating effect. The Luftwaffe had notably used them to cause substantial damage and casualties during the Clydeside Blitz from 13–15 March 1941. The blast damage when these mines exploded was far greater than if a normal bomb had hit the ground, as much of the blast is directed upwards. The effect on anyone within a radius of up to hundreds of metres (depending on the size of the air mine) was deadly as the damage was caused not so much by debris from the bomb or its fragments but by the shock wave that was created by the blast, which caused lungs to explode and eardrums to burst, as well as causing massive internal injuries of the type found in some members of the Dyatlov group. There is a strong possibility that the two Tu-95M 'Bears' had dropped the air mines and that they were either dropped in the wrong location or the parachutes were blown off course due to the strong winds known to have been present during that period.

The worst of the injuries caused to three of the group would have been explained by a military accident of this nature. Although it does not explain Luda Dubinina's missing tongue, it is quite possible that she could have bitten it off and her body may have been cleaned before it was moved, as her mouth and face would most likely have shown traces of a great deal of blood. There was no mention in the autopsy report of any traces of blood, despite her tongue being missing, although the autopsy did record the coagulated blood in her stomach. The car-crash type injuries without external marks, which were recorded for three of the group, could have been caused by a blast from an air mine. Explosive blasts of this nature can cause internal damage, including broken ribs, without leaving any external marks. For example, a number of the victims of the 2005 London tube and bus bombings had died of internal injuries caused by the blasts, without any external markings or even scratches.

Thermobaric weapons

Tied in with the above theory of the Tu-95M 'Bear' air mines is the suggestion that the worst internal injuries to Luda Dubinina, Semyon Zolotarev and Nicolai Thibeaux-Brignolle were caused by a 'vacuum bomb'.

A 'vacuum bomb' is one of a group of names of these types of bombs (others are: HITs – high impulse thermobaric weapons; fuel air explosives; heat and pressure weapons), which applies to what are known as thermobaric weapons. These include fuel–air bombs and are distinguished from other types of bombs by producing a blast wave that lasts considerably longer than condensed explosives used in other weaponry. The longer blast wave from a thermobaric bomb causes significantly more damage and casualties. A thermobaric explosion relies on oxygen from the surrounding air, compared with normal explosives that are made up of a fuel–oxidiser premix. What happens on ignition is that a flame accelerates to a large volume, which produces pressure fronts within the mixture of fuel and oxidant in the surrounding air. A thermobaric bomb would normally be a container packed with a fuel substance, in the middle of which is a small conventional explosive 'scatter charge'. A strong container would allow the fuel to be contained long enough for it to be heated to well above its automatic ignition temperature, so that even the cooling of it during its expansion from the container results in rapid ignition once the mixture is within conventional flammability limits. The description of the 'vacuum bomb' comes from when the gases cool and the pressure rapidly drops, leading to a vacuum that can be powerful enough to damage buildings and people.

Research into this group of weapons was initially started by the Germans during the Second World War, using coal dust as fuel; development was continued by both the USA and the USSR. The weapons were used by the Americans in the Vietnam War and more recently in Afghanistan. The Soviet military also used these weapons in the Sino-Soviet conflict, Afghanistan and in post-Communist Russia in the Chechen conflict. An interesting point about thermobaric explosives is that they can be used in a hand grenade with a lethal radius of only 10m, up to massive bombs with a lethal radius of 2km.

The casualties of these weapons are either obliterated by the fireball at the centre of ignition or by the shock wave coming out of it. The injuries sustained include ruptures to the lungs and internal organs, shattered eardrums and crushed inner ear organs, and severe concussion. Many of these injuries are described as 'invisible injuries', which fits into the descriptions of the worst injuries to Luda Dubinina, Semyon Zolotarev and Nicolai Thibeaux-Brignolle – with possible internal damage also to the others but these not being mentioned in the autopsy in order to try and cover up what had happened.

The problem with this theory, as with the infrasound theory, is that an explanation for the injuries has been found but without a link to say exactly when and how the injuries came to be caused by a weapon of this nature. Again, similar to the suggestion that the group was close to or had gone into the northern military testing area, a thermobaric weapon may have been used that accidentally killed some or all of the members of the group, possibly causing concussions that left the remaining members of the group so disabled that they froze to death. One point against the thermobaric weapon theory is that as these explosives rely on atmospheric oxygen, they do not work underwater, at high altitudes or in bad weather. The last two items both apply to the Dyatlov group scenario.

Political theory[1]

Whilst this theory does not involve a different location for the actual deaths, it is included in this chapter as a major part of the events involves another location on the Dyatlov route.

There is no question that the trip by the Dyatlov group had political overtones. They were making their trip in honour of the 21st Communist Party Congress and while none of them were highly connected within the Communist Party, they were nevertheless considered to be good examples of the young communist ideal. After it became apparent to relatives and friends in Sverdlovsk that something was seriously wrong and no word had been heard from the group, concerned relatives started to make complaints to the Communist Party authorities in Sverdlovsk, and through them to more senior officials in Moscow. It has been said that the Premier Nikita Khrushchev himself gave an order that no effort was to be spared in finding the missing group. Accordingly, this would probably explain why four specialists in this type of search and rescue operations were sent from Moscow at very short notice to assist.

However, a theory was put forward in September 2011 by Alexander Gulikov. The underlying theme of this theory, once again, is set against the background of the Soviet Union and the way it was run in 1959. What was happening during that time seems almost incomprehensible to someone in the current day, looking back and wondering why something that would seem perhaps not so unusual today, would be taken as treasonable behaviour in those times. The theory involves a power fight between some of the top Communist Party bosses in Moscow.

During that period, the 21st Communist Party Congress was taking place in Moscow. When major events such as a Party Congress were held, orders were usually issued by respective ministries (the Interior, the Navy, the KGB, etc) to place them on what was known as an enhanced service mode, when it was strictly prohibited for any military hardware to leave its location, any personnel training connected with the taking out of military hardware is cancelled, soldiers cannot go on leave, neither can officers go on leave, and commanders are on round-the-clock duty.

During the 21st Communist Party Congress in Moscow, military officers who were friendly with at least one of the top Moscow bosses had gone hunting in the valley of the River Auspia. The group also had Mansi hunters to act as beaters. (A group of Mansi beaters would act together to flush out wildlife and game towards the line of approaching hunters.) The return from the hunt was planned for 1 February 1959. For their return they used a military helicopter, which on the face of it did not seem too great a crime for military officers even though they were using it for personal reasons and it was in contravention of an order that forbade the use of such equipment. However, it is suggested that the KGB were fully aware of what was happening and a plan was conceived and put into action under instructions from certain party bosses in Moscow in order to discredit another party boss.

A working plan of the operation was thoroughly developed, and personnel were appointed to supervise the operation. A camera was prepared with a special film and a system of recording the date and time of every shot. The camera was sealed in the presence of the supervisor of the operation. With such a system, the shots could be acknowledged as evidence only with the seal being intact. Also, clothes were prepared and marked with radio isotopes. The operator, who would take the photographs, had to wrap the camera in those clothes and leave them with the camera in an agreed place once he had finished his task. It is suggested that such a place may have been near the Dyatlov storage shed. After that, the camera had to be taken away as soon as possible. The clothes marked with radio isotopes were to help with detecting the location of the camera. The operator for the camera was appointed: Semyon Zolotarev. In Gulikov's opinion, this was not a man called Zolotarev at all. He feels that 'Zolotarev's' biography is extremely vague and tangled. Also the confusion with finalising the eventual list of the group leaving on the Dyatlov group hike is connected with the appearance of this person. He was a stranger in the group. Gulikov does not know if he was a career officer of the KGB. It may be that he was not, but he may have been useful to them. Gulikov points out (as many others have done) the fact of Zolotarev's burial at a prestigious cemetery in Sverdlovsk, separately from the rest of the Dyatlov group.

Gulikov also feels that there was an effort to crack down on misuse of equipment, as well as the attempt to discredit someone by linking him with using his friends in high places (i.e. a top Moscow party boss) to do what he wanted with military equipment, in this case personal hunting with friends. The prime objective, though, was to discredit the Moscow party boss rather than the high-ranking military officer who was misusing military equipment.

Zolotarev would not have known the real reasons why he was taking the photographs. However, Gulikov's premise is that Zolotarev was spotted taking photos. This observation of him started a chain of events leading to the elimination of the whole group and this explains why there was so much secrecy in the course of the investigation and the large number of senior officials from different services who had made their appearance at the pass during the course of rescue operations.

The operation began with ensuring that the Dyatlov group appeared in the Taiga by a certain date when the helicopter would be there. In Gulikov's opinion, information about the date of the helicopter flight was brought to the second severny by a Mansi hunter. The group had started making good progress but after Yudin had left to return and the group had left the second severny, further movement was surprisingly slow. Zina Kolmogorova wrote in her diary for 30 January about 'slowly getting up' in the morning. They resumed their journey only at about 10 a.m. or even later. There was no need for them to hurry as they knew they were making good time. Also, Mansi trails were everywhere in the area as they (the Mansi) were preparing the hunt for the military officers. On 31 January the Dyatlov group left the ski track and moved up to the edge of the forest, moving away from the Auspia and wading through virgin snow, then they returned back to the river valley. This manoeuvre was evidently going around something. The 'something' was the military officers; Igor Dyatlov writes about this in the group's diary ('the move away from the Auspia and back again').

The supposition is that Zolotarev was seen taking photographs as the helicopter was in the air. As the helicopter returned to Ivdel, Zolotarev (and maybe one more person – possibly Dyatlov) quickly returned back to the group. The group then packed everything and in great haste moved to another, less convenient place, making a camp at the foot of Kholat Syakhl in the hope they would not be found. Zolotarev did not hide the camera with the isotope-marked clothes, his task was to leave those things near the shed.

On their return, the officers realised that photos have been taken of their illegal use of the helicopter. They send trusted men back in the helicopter to find the group and do whatever it took to bring the cameras back.

These men found the tourists' camp on the mountain slope on 1 February, at some distance from the place where the group had been noticed earlier. The helicopter landed either at the River Lozva from where they went to the tent following the ski trail, or nearer, on the slope. Even though the instructions were to do without bloodshed, they probably met with resistance by the group (who did not understand what was happening, except for Zolotarev and probably Dyatlov) and a fight broke out. The military men were well versed in unarmed combat and knew how to kill without leaving external marks.

The military men could not have known that the operation involving the taking of photographs was under the control of the KGB. Zolotarev would have felt assured of the strength of the organisation behind him and did not want to give them the camera. Events probably got out of hand very quickly and when the military men saw that they had overdone things, their decision was to leave no one alive.

Gulikov estimates that at about 6–7 a.m. the next day (2 February), these men returned and, using their broad skis, they cleared up leaving no tracks in the soft snow. They found the dead bodies, but not all in one place. It was then that they searched out the bodies of Dyatlov and the other two, Krivonischenko and Doroshenko, under the cedar. They found Dubinina and Zolotarev still alive and killed them by pressing on the carotid artery with the use of *obmotki* (puttees), then threw them down the snow hole (the shelter it was believed they had tried to build). One of these puttees was later found near the cedar and another one in the gulley.

The military officers and their men, along with the helicopter crew, felt they were in deep trouble. The issue of the illegal use of the helicopter was now about to be disclosed. On top of this, all the members of the Dyatlov group were dead. It was therefore in the interests of everybody concerned (the various services and ministries) to hush up the whole story. The situation with regard to the power struggle in Moscow was shifted to the backburner. The party leaders did not want the story to become known to the general public and, worst of all, to be leaked to the foreign press. The top military leaders wanted to find the camera but they didn't know where it was. The KGB wanted to find the camera, but without the interference of the military.

Gulikov goes on to state some points: the resulting investigation was protracted. Gulikov felt that Lev Ivanov (the lead investigator on the case) had by the conclusion of the case known how the Dyatlov group had been eliminated and who had killed them. However, he was given a categorical order to close the case, and he wrote a considered and bland conclusion that allowed him to do so. Tempalov's Mansi version was discarded. The criminal version was completely excluded.

To complete Gulikov's theory: the camera found on Zolotarev in May by the military was taken to Sverdlovsk, what happened to it after it was examined is unknown. There was no compromising material in the camera regarding the Dyatlov group, but the illegal use of a military helicopter came out.

To summarise, Gulikov notes (as many others have done) the absurd conclusions of the investigation, the complete dropping of facts so clearly pointing to a criminal act and, finally at the end, the territory was closed to tourists for a number of years. Gulikov also points to the lack of evidence of an avalanche, a failed missile launch and no blast damage anywhere at the scene, and when the spring thaw started, there were no dead birds or animals from any blast. He also mentions the evidence of multiple unidentified footprints.

Finally, he felt that the answer to the mystery and conclusive proof of his theory lies in the Ural Military District archives where there must be information about what had happened in 1959. Also there would be information in the archives of the KGB (now the FSB) and that the Russian Ministry of Defence must have internal investigation material on the use of military equipment for personal purposes, with respective conclusions and proposals of sanctions. It must be said here that the use of a military helicopter for a short private flight in 1959 would be small change compared with what happened after the break-up of the USSR when nearly everything seemed to be up for grabs and whole large transport aircraft seemed to disappear into thin air. Nonetheless, there still may be information on such a helicopter flight if the material can be accessed.

Finally, Alexander Gulikov is of the opinion that it would be worthwhile to test out the avalanche theory under the same conditions at the pass, in winter if possible.

Gennady Kisilov comments on investigation

Another source who strongly disputed the official version of events and also disputed the place where the deaths took place is Gennady Kisilov. At the time of writing (2012), he was an old age pensioner who lived in the closed city of Novouralsk, where prior to his retirement he worked at a large chemical factory that processed weapons-grade plutonium. He gathered together a group of individuals who set about thoroughly investigating the deaths of the Dyatlov group.

What Kisilov did was to go through the whole investigation from start to finish. This included a complete analysis of all the documents (it must be stressed here that these were the documents that are currently available as opposed to any other documents which may be withheld) of the criminal case, the transcripts of the interrogations of rescuers and relatives of the hikers, and all published material that covered the incident in the mass media. The new facts he brought to light may not be regarded as indisputable, but he made a serious and determined, as well as an unbiased, attempt to try and get to the bottom of the story. As well as conducting his own investigations, what emerged from his digging were a number of interpretations of the facts which changed what he felt was a 'vicious circle' surrounding the theories in the public arena in the last twenty years in the search for a solution to the mystery. He felt that the 'vicious circle', as he named it, was the concentration only on the official theories relating to the deaths (i.e. avalanche, wild animals, escaped prisoners, etc). The following is a summary of the main points raised by Kisilov.

Kisilov first focused on what he called the 'DIEs' (Dyatlov Incident Experts), people who relied solely on the statement of Lev Ivanov, the man initially in charge of the case. This statement by Ivanov is dated 28 May 1959 on the termination of the criminal case into the Dyatlov group deaths. Kisilov's in-depth analysis of this document threw up very few truthful assertions. He also pointed out a number of witness statements that were contradictory and his opinion was that overall the document simply could not be relied on to be used as a guide to what had really happened. He said that a first brief overview of the documents gave a number of indications of how the presence of 'outsiders' (i.e. the search parties) on the search scene (the slopes of Kholat Syakhl and surrounding vicinity) basically created so much confusion and chaos that it would have been impossible to work out exactly what had happened at the tent before the arrival of the other search parties. For instance, not a single footprint in the snow had been properly identified with any of the Dyatlov group's footprints. No such task had been assigned to anyone during the course of the investigation. To summarise: the tent was spotted and members of the search party started trampling around the scene and moving around it as well as moving up and down the mountain where the other tracks were. Despite this confusion, it should have been possible to differentiate between the older and the newer tracks, but with more and more additional movement around the scene, many of the tracks were obliterated. In fairness to the search parties, they expected to still find the members of the Dyatlov group alive at this point. The question must be asked as to why there was a definitive statement made regarding the tracks only of nine people. Kisilov considered the mention in the documents of '8 to 9 pairs of footprints'[2] to be irrelevant; he felt that this particular detail should be of no consequence and therefore ignored completely.

Another most significant piece of information arose from the testimony of a navigator of an An-2. This navigator was named Karpushin and if one takes Karpushin's testimony as the truth, it destroys the basis of the version of the official investigation documents. On 25 February, Karpushin was flying over the area in an An-2. He was observing the ground when he saw from the air a tent with its side cut into what he described as 'rags'. This fact alone is of paramount importance, since on the morning of 26 February, the leader of the search party that first reached the tent, Slobtsov with his fellow rescuers, saw the same tent with a slashed side, but only after the team had dug the tent from underneath compacted snow. The weather was fine on 25 February: sunshine, no precipitation. Then the very next day there suddenly appeared a layer of compacted snow of 5–7in (15–20cm) thick on the collapsed tent. What made the tent 'fall' under snow literally overnight?

Kisilov's view was that this snow on top of the collapsed tent could have only come from one source and that was from what he described as the 'fake scene organisers'. In other words, the whole site had been set up to appear as if this was where the group had made their camp and subsequently had met their deaths from this site.

By removing the far prop of the roof ridge, which was some distance from the entrance, they dropped the tent, after having first placed the Dyatlov group's belongings and equipment inside, and then covered it up with snow. The impression that the tent had been there for three weeks under snow had therefore been successful, since for ten to fifteen years afterwards, many of the DIEs had not even remotely guessed that the tent had appeared on the scene only a couple of days before it was discovered. A further point made by another observer of the photograph taken of the tent immediately after it was discovered is that the supporting skis that held the ridge of the tent in place with a line going from one ski to another, supporting the middle of the tent, was that the skis had been placed at the ends of the tent (i.e. lengthways) whereas for maximum support and to shorten the distance, the skis should have been placed on each side of the tent (i.e. widthways). Earlier pictures taken from the Dyatlov group's cameras show a picture of the tent taken earlier on the trip, which shows the tent being supported widthways, not lengthways. This is a strong indication that the tent had been put in place by others.

Another item that stood out was the matter of the Chinese-made flashlight, which was found on top of the tent. This puzzled the first rescue party (Slobtsov's) when they saw it, because the flashlight was found lying on a 1–3.5in (5–10cm) layer of snow, but there was no snow on the torch itself. Kisilov felt that in an attempt to give some kind of authenticity to the scene, the 'stage-hands' who were setting the scene were experienced enough to try and concentrate on some detail and had thrown the flashlight onto the collapsed tent, to make it look as though the flashlight had been dropped in haste. The only problem being, of course, that as this had only been done not long before the arrival of the search parties, there had been no time for snow to collect on it, as the previous day had been clear.

There were also a few other inconsistencies: there was a back-prop for the tent that was completely missing; a trace of urine was found near the tent; a damaged ski pole was found lying inside the tent over the personal items of the group. As previously mentioned, Yury Yudin had confirmed that no one in the group had such a pole, which had cuts on the end of it.

Kisilov's conclusions were that as far as the scene around the tent was concerned, the DIEs had missed many things. Following on from Navigator Karpushin's statement regarding the tent and bodies he observed on 25 February, a member of a geological party named Titov was flying over the same area the previous day on 24 February and looking for ski tracks, but had not seen a tent (neither a tent corner sticking out from snow nor a standing tent with a visible slashed side). It means there was no tent there at the time

Titov flew over. It must be deduced from this that the tent was brought and set up at some point after Titov had flown over, probably on 24 February as Karpushin observed it on the following morning on 25 February. Karpushin was actually flying in the same An-2 as Titov, as it was the only An-2 aircraft in Ivdel.

In addition to seeing the tent, Navigator Karpushin also saw two bodies, male and female, lying on the snow very close to the tent. Although Karpushin had seen the tent and the two bodies from the air on 25 February, in the morning of 26 February there were no bodies there. At least we know that no bodies were reported by Slobtsov's rescue team when they first arrived on the scene. However, this evidence cannot be totally trusted. It may well be that a dead body was found when they looked inside the tent, since, according to the testimony of George Atmanaki, Slobtsov's search party was absolutely exhausted and close to incapacitation in the last days of February due to the stresses they had suffered, particularly in the first two days of frantic searching.

Karpushin was required to sign a non-disclosure agreement, along with the pilot of the An-2 (named Patrushev) and a number of others. Karpushin said nothing for years but finally gave an interview at the age of 81 in 2004 to the newspaper *AIF-URAL*. This is the only place that Karpushin's version has appeared and, despite been instructed to sign a non-disclosure agreement, there is no mention of his testimony in the official criminal investigation of the case.

If the sighting of the two bodies near the tent as reported by Karpushin on 25 February is correct, then it would be quite apparent that there was no 'rush escape from the Mountain of the Dead'[3] as given in the official version of events, but rather to the possibility that the bodies of the

Dyatlov group had been transported to the slopes of Kholat Syakhl, rather than they had made their own way there. The possibility could exist that the two bodies seen by Karpushin had met their end at the tent or nearby, but then why move them to where they were eventually found?

Another scenario is that the bodies were brought to two 'unloading points': the tent and the cedar tree. A further point made in relation to the possible movement of the bodies is the presence of 'improvised ropes'[4] of twisted strips of cloth or plaits that were found in the tent but not described in any great detail in the inventory made of the items found. These were not medical tourniquets and Kisilov felt that these were used to assist the movement of the bodies in blankets, using these 'improvised ropes'.

In relation to the two bodies, everything hinges on Karpushin's evidence. Despite the potential flaws and lack of confirmation of Karpushin's testimony, it is not vital to the theory that the bodies were brought to Kholat Syakhl from somewhere else. Equally, the question of the area from where the Dyatlov group's bodies had been brought from to the slopes of Kholat Syakhl remains open. The criminal investigation was opened on 6 February but it seems (if one agrees with Karpushin's observations) that the scene was being prepared and the placing of the bodies was being carried out on 25 February, so there would have been a considerable time gap with this scenario. It is known that the approximate place of the catastrophe was in the general area of Mount Otorten, but it seems that the dead and/or half-dead Dyatlov group had been taken away from the site of the tragedy immediately, but where had they been moved to?

The possible answer to this question may be found in the testimony by Yury Yudin. According to him, even before the deaths of the Dyatlov group became known back at the university in Sverdlovsk, the digging for potentially compromising evidence was already under way and a rumour started (by the Trade Union Committee at the university) to circulate that, allegedly, they had tried to escape abroad and had lost their lives in extreme conditions during the attempt. Kisilov's view was that for this rumour to have some credence, the bodies of the group would not be found on the slopes of Kholat Syakhl but rather two days' travelling distance away, approximately 25 miles (40km) north of Mount Otorten so as to appear that the whole group was attempting to make some kind of escape out of the Soviet Union. In 1959 it was impossible for a Soviet citizen to just leave the country of their own accord. The possible reasoning for this route is that it would have been easier to escape from the north than from the more heavily guarded and policed areas to the south and west. As unlikely as this scenario might appear, should it have been believed, then their names would have been defamed, the UPI leadership would have been dismissed from their posts and their university friends would have been mentioning their names with disgust. However, the fabricated rumours of the escape attempt were treated with derision and the story basically did not 'work'. As a little time elapsed for these rumours to start taking effect, it therefore became necessary for another scenario to be developed and developed quickly. The dead bodies were therefore moved to another search scene, which had to be prepared in a very short time prior to the arrival of the search teams.

Kisilov believes that a search scenario and a plan involving the 'discovery' of dead bodies were rapidly put together and approved at the headquarters of the CPSU (Communist Party of the Soviet Union) Central Committee and the Oblast Committee (regional administration). This plan was then followed through to its final conclusions, resulting in the eventual Criminal Investigation Report.

The next area that Kisilov concentrated on was the presence of so many senior officials, including both civil and military prior to and during the search. Going back to navigator Karpushin's testimony, Kisilov found that in addition to mentioning the significant detail regarding the observation of the torn tent and two bodies on 25 February, Karpushin spoke of the presence of a military general in Ivdel who controlled the search operation. On further investigation it appeared there was more than one general in Ivdel during the search and this was mentioned by a number of sources, including: V. Strauch, a student of local history; Investigator Vladimir Korotayev; G.Grigoryev, a special correspondent of the *Uralsky Rabochy* (Urals Worker) newspaper; A. Gushchin, a journalist on the newspaper *Oblastnaya Gazeta*.

Beside the presence of military generals in Ivdel, testimonies examined by Kisilov also uncovered the fact that there were a number of other senior officials there at the same time, including members of the Communist Party Central Committee, the Communist Party Oblast Committee and members of the Extraordinary Commission (see below) and the UPI leadership.

The First Secretary of the Ivdel Communist Party City Committee, I.S. Prodanov, was named as the 'official' search supervisor. In reality, however, he was nothing more than a front behind which the real players were hidden. There was one significant inclusion to the group of people organising the search. This was Yevgeny Maslennikov, a Master of Sports in Tourism (a high Soviet sports ranking), who made some radical alterations to the search plan. Maslennikov formulated a plan to land rescue teams along the whole length of the Dyatlov group's possible route, which on the face of it seemed to be a good idea, but Kisilov's opinion is that this plan was used to basically turn the whole search campaign into an unco-ordinated mess. Maslennikov died in

1983 and had kept a diary (or collection of diaries) of the events. This diary (or diaries) is now in a private archive, although people who have seen it say that it is exaggerated.

Maslennikov's proposals to land the rescue teams along the route was approved by the CPSU Oblast Committee. The decision was then made to activate the search teams and they were landed at different points on 26 February. This is despite the fact that the tent had already been seen from the air by Karpushin the previous day, but had not yet been 'found' by the team of students led by Slobtsov, which was according to the plan formulated by Maslennikov and the Oblast Committee. At 6 p.m. Moscow time (8 p.m. local time) on 26 February a report came into the search headquarters in Ivdel about the discovery of the tent by Slobtsov's group, and the following day about 40 rescuers from other points of the Dyatlov group's route were then directed to where the tent was found on Kholat Syakhl. Without even a preliminary briefing or the correct supervision of a public prosecutor, the result of all these additional searchers descending on the tent at the same time was complete disorder and led to an initial investigation of the scene being carried out by curious and eager but totally incompetent students. The mess at the scene that had been started by Slobtsov's group was continued by the whole 'army' of searchers, which played into the hands of the people behind the scenes. The implication here is that the chaos about to be created at the tent was the intention of the Oblast Communist Party Committee and was carried out with their approval.

The first people connected with the search to appear in Ivdel were Lev Gordo, the head of the UPI tourist club, and Yury Blinov, a UPI student and leader of the tourist group that started on a hike together with the Dyatlov group. The two groups had travelled together as far as the 41st Kvartal before the Yury Blinov group headed off on a route further south to that taken by the Dyatlov group.

At this stage Lev Gordo sensed that a threat of punishment was hanging over him for having missed the target date of the Dyatlov group return, and he had started a rumour that Dyatlov had sent word with Yury Yudin (who returned on account of his illness) that the target date was being moved back to a later date because the group was behind schedule. At best this was an exaggeration and at worst it was an outright lie, because when the Dyatlov group parted with Yudin at the second severny it was actually one day ahead of the schedule planned by Igor Dyatlov. This fact can be easily checked. Given the average rate of progress on the route at 12 miles (20km) per day, the 37 miles (60km) distance from Vizhay (the starting point) to the second severny (the abandoned geologist settlement) could be covered in three days by the group moving on skis. But, by using the passing transport, they saved one day and arrived at the second severny late in the evening of 27 January. So, travelling on skis and following Igor Dyatlov's original schedule, the group had planned to leave the second severny on 29 January, but actually left the village the day before, on 28 January. Regarding the whole of the original schedule, the group was making excellent progress and was already a total of three days ahead. They were supposed to leave Vizhay on the original start date of 28 January, but on this date they were actually leaving the second severny located at a distance of three days' passage. This issue of time and progress is relatively minor but is used by Kisilov to show that Lev Gordo was wrong in what he had said; it also serves to highlight an overall impression that the authorities would have been quite happy for everyone to think that the Dyatlov group was hopelessly behind schedule and that blame could not be apportioned for a failure to act sooner in the search for them.

Despite any errors that Lev Gordo had made, he was considered by the students to be a very decent man. When the inevitable retribution came, he was dismissed from his post along with the university rector. Many people, including students at the university, considered the punishments to be harsh and unfair.

At the Ivdel airfield on the afternoon of 23 February, the Slobtsov search team comprising nine students was divided into two groups. They left at the same time and were then flown in two Mi-8 helicopters to two different start points. The search group of four students (including Slobtsov) and two guides (a total of six people) were brought to the eastern part of the Mount Otorten ridge. The other search group of five students were landed on the bank of the lower course of the River Auspia.

Almost nothing is known of the activities of the first search group in the period from 23–25 February, before the groups came together on the River Auspia. The second search group had seen a fire with people gathered around it on the lower side of the slope of Kholat Syakhl. The search group stopped there for the night; probably they had met with what they described as 'outsiders' (believed to be KGB officers on the search).

The second search party then started making their way upstream along the River Auspia. They had found and were following what they described as 'hardly visible narrow ski tracks'. On 25 February both groups came together again; now the team numbered eleven people in total, including the guides.

On the River Auspia, Slobtsov's group had allegedly discovered an 'earlier' Dyatlov camp. Soon, not far from the first one, some Mansi searchers found another 'earlier' Dyatlov camp. It remains unknown when exactly the camps were discovered. In Kisilov's opinion, the 'hardly visible' narrow ski tracks and both of the 'earlier' Dyatlov camps were the result of what he described as 'outsider' activities.

At a meeting at the headquarters in Ivdel, Ortyukov and Maslennikov both mentioned a southern group team that was supposed to start from the second severny and then move up the River Lozva to meet up with Slobtsov's search group. It is believed that this mysterious southern search team was composed of KGB officers, as there is no other reference to them and they were not students or Mansi.

Kisilov goes on to describe the 'contrived' discovery of the Dyatlov tent.

On 26 February, the guides led part of Slobtsov's group to 'discover' the Dyatlov group's tent. The group of 'discoverers' consisted of five people: Slobtsov, Brusnitsyn, Sharavin, and two guides, Cheglakov and Pashin. The tent was 'discovered', but here the official investigation rather bizarrely describes the behaviour of the three students as the Russian equivalent of 'went off their trollies': they were described as complaining of serious stress, fatigue and incapacitation.

Early in March, the storage shed was at last found. A correct protocol or procedure of discovery was established and compiled by the lead prosecutor on the case, Lev Ivanov, on 2 March, while the actual discovery proper took place late in the evening on 3 March, in dark and blizzard conditions. Kisilov believes this discovery to be almost certainly a fake, with the mix-up in dates pointing to it.

There were a couple of smaller points made by Kisilov that he felt to be worthy of note. The first involved the man appointed as leader of the overall search campaign, Yevgeny Maslennikov. He had arrived in Ivdel burning with enthusiasm to search for the Dyatlov group and find out what had happened to them. Within one week of his arrival, he asked if he could be released and allowed to go home. In other words, once the tent was found, he appeared to lose all interest. It could be said that once the tent had been found along with the first bodies, his job was done, but considering the condition of the tent and where the bodies were found, the job was really only just beginning.

The other point was something mentioned by Moses Akselrod at his interrogation. Akselrod was a student at UPI and knew the members of the Dyatlov group well. He was involved in the search and had helped to sort out the belongings and equipment found in the tent. He saw the handwritten original of the group's *Evening Otorten* paper and Zolotarev's diary, because he compared Zolotarev's handwriting with the paper and found they were both the same. This does not seem particularly relevant on its own but it has relevance in another theory, which involves Zolotarev being part of a conspiracy that was unknown to the others in the group, with Zolotarev writing about a snowman – implying a creature was in the vicinity (see Chapter 6).

As an aside, Kisilov mentions that on 5 March 1959, after the first bodies had been found, an 'Extraordinary Commission for Rescue Operations' was formed under the auspices of the Sverdlovsk Oblast Communist Party Committee by I.S. Prodanov, the Secretary General of the Ivdel Communist Party Committee. This 'Extraordinary Commission' included two other senior officials (Pavlov and Philip Yermash) and Investigator Vladimir Korotayev said that this Extraordinary Commission for Rescue Operations 'drank hard'[5] in the village of Pershino on the River Lozva. It was said that this was probably their 'Special Mission'.[6]

Kisilov felt that there are still many questions left unanswered and made the observation that there are actually only two people living today who may have information: the former investigator of the Ivdel prosecutor's office, Vladimir Korotayev, and the former leader of the search party that found the tent, Boris Slobtsov. (NB: this was at the time of Kisilov's writing – Korotayev died on 11 July 2012.)

8

What happened – the Yury Yakimov theory

Yury Yakimov was a shift foreman from Severouralsk (a city in the north Urals, 178km (110 miles) from the Dyatlov Pass). His theory attempts to explain the nature of the injuries, the strange behaviour and many other inconsistencies in the story of the Dyatlov group and is based on the author's personal encounter with an unexplained phenomenon, which took place during a night shift in an open-pit mine in 2002. The following – the remainder of this chapter – is a translated and condensed account in his own words.

On 11 September 2002 I was working as a night-shift foreman at the Ivdelsky unit of the Bauxite mine. The night shifts generally lasted 12 hours, from 9 p.m. to 9 a.m. At the time, we conducted operations at several sites located quite far away from each other (up to 12km between the sites). The mining equipment in No. 15 pit was at a standstill from the beginning of the shift because our trucks were all busy carrying ore from the No. 3 ore dump to the ore stockpile near Ivdel railway station. These distant sites were quite far away from the pit, and the No. 15 pit with the installed equipment was located beside the main road over which the trucks transported ore. There were no people in the pit from the beginning of the shift, and the equipment was unguarded.

Shortly after I started on this particular shift, it was getting dark. I went to switch on the electric lights in the pit to illuminate the southern part of the No. 15 pit and examine the equipment. There had been numerous thefts in the pits during that period, when thieves cut and carried away power cables, took wires off the power transmission lines and stole ferrous metal items to sell them to scrap collectors. As I mentioned, equipment in the pits was unguarded and so shift foremen had to keep an eye on the equipment as well as get on with their work.

It was 11 p.m. and dark and I was walking down the road leading to No. 15 pit. I was already near the transformer from which I could turn on the floodlights to illuminate the pit, when approximately 200m away from me I saw a strange shaking white light moving up and down the side of a rock dump. It was as if someone was sitting in a car with halogen headlights and was moving it around wildly. The light bounced up and down the side of the dump. The distance from the source of the light to the side of the dump that it was illuminating was about 100m. There was not a single sound, only leaves rustling in a slight breeze, and a little drizzling rain started falling.

Suddenly a beam of light from the unknown source started turning in my direction and shone on me across the forest. I rushed off the road and ran to the transformer (it stood at the roadside), opened the transformer box door and turned on the lighting in the pit. Lamps then illuminated the southern part of the pit, but the broad beam of light from the unknown source continued shining on me. It flooded the whole of the forest around me with a bright white light. The light itself was as bright as day and it seemed as if the trees had no shadows.

I stood behind the electrical box, near the transformer, with my face turned away. There were two or three minutes of agonising suspense, then the broad beam of bright white light slowly moved away from me. Everything was still quiet.

I looked again in the direction of the source of the strange light and saw how the beam of light from the source again started moving towards me. I noticed a couple of flashlights had separated from the source and were moving in my direction. At first there were two of them and they seemed to be swinging. They moved fairly quickly across the forest towards me. I turned away then looked up again. Now there were four or five of them, maybe more. They struggled through the forest as if enveloping tree trunks. It was as if several people with strong torches were moving through the thick forest trying to spot me. Unintentionally, I looked away again and froze. Immediately the torches left me alone. There was something very strange going on.

These were certainly not thieves. It was something different, very strange and unusual. I realised that I had witnessed an amazing and unusual phenomenon. Clearly, this source of light seemed to react to my glance, it dazzled me with its light and sent the swinging torches in my direction. When I turned or looked away to where the source of light could not be seen, the torches did not react to me. Nor did they react to the lamps (two of them) that illuminated the southern part of the pit.

I went down the temporary exit road in the western part of the pit and examined the shovel and the feeder cable. Everything was intact. There were no tracks of a vehicle either in the pit or on the road near the pit. The road was wet after the rain and any track would have been visible. There were no other roads leading to this pit.

While down in the pit I kept thinking of the unusual dancing lights. What were they? Where did they come from? Why did they react to my glance?

As I was leaving the pit I again saw the continuing dancing of light on the side of the rock dump. I looked to the right, in the direction of its source, and again a beam of light immediately came in my direction. The same thing was happening again. There was no doubt. The source of light appeared to react to a human glance.

It was something I could not explain. I felt weird from the strangeness of what I had seen and I felt anxious and uneasy. To put on a show of bravado, I shouted as loud as I could, 'Hey! Hello! What's up?' Then I whistled and cursed. But the inexplicable light phenomenon did not react either to my curses, or to the whistling.

And then, from far away, the wind brought the roar of an approaching heavy loaded truck. There was no reaction from the source of unusual light to this sound.

I looked again at the light dancing on the side of the dump. Once again, a beam of light from the source came in my direction. I did not want to tempt fate any longer and left the place. I walked to the fork of the main road and soon the truck with a load of ore appeared. I climbed into the cabin and told the driver what I had just seen. I felt he was wary of what I was saying, but I didn't try to convince him or prove anything. I felt extremely tired, sluggish and jaded. Probably it was because I couldn't get rid of the feeling of anxiety and danger that I felt as a result of the strange light.

As usual, after midnight at 1 a.m., the shift workers gathered in the canteen. I told them about what I saw in the No. 15 pit. Their reaction was of the sort, 'We would be happy to believe you, but what you are saying is just too incredible. Perhaps it was your imagination?'

Who knows? I personally would not have believed it if someone else had told me such a story.

But I had seen it and I could not just get it out of my head. For a brief moment I even had a crazy idea to go back there, to the pit, to break through to that source of light and see what there was behind it all. But the feeling of anxiety and danger from what I had seen did not leave me, and I gave up the idea.

For the rest of the night the trucks continued carrying ore from the No. 3 intermediate ore dump to the railway station stockpile and did not stop off near the No. 15 pit where I had seen the unusual light.

In the morning at about 7 a.m., when dawn had already broken, the trucks started carrying ore from the No. 15 pit to the ore dump. No tracks of other cars or vehicles could be seen after the night rain on the wet road leading to the No. 15 pit. There was not a trace near the place where I had watched the unusual light source either.

Where the light had come from and how it had appeared in the No. 15 pit – and where it had gone – remained unclear. It left no trace of its presence. Everyone refused to believe me when I tried to tell them what had happened. 'This is just your imagination. Things do happen sometimes ...' Should I have tried once again to prove that I was not seeing things? But what did I have in order to prove what I was saying? No tracks and no evidence. Eventually I stopped thinking about it.

After a few days, the story of the light that had reacted to a human glance was almost forgotten.

Then, after a week or two, late in September 2002, I got a copy of the newspaper *Za boksity*. I had been subscribing to the paper for several years. The paper came with a supplement entitled *Ecoved*, dated September 2002, No. 9/29, and it gave information about the Denezhkin Kamen nature reserve located in the territory of the Severouralsk district.

Under the heading 'News from Forest Cordon', I read this:

An unusual phenomenon has been reported by Reserve Forest Rangers V Yefimov and VS Rudkovsky when they were returning from their inspection round of the Yelovsky Ridge.

At 9pm the rangers' attention was attracted by a bright electrical light 'as if from a projector' directed from west to east. One of the eyewitnesses described the unusual phenomenon: 'I looked harder and saw that it looked as if two people were moving in my direction holding torches. The weather was clear and it was quiet. I decided to get nearer and see who it might be. When I was about 5 or 10 metres from the fire the number of torches suddenly increased to seven. I hid behind a Cedar and cautiously looked out, but was immediately dazzled with the light coming as if from a projector. There was some 'set' in front of me which, for some reason or other, reacted to a glance only, and in no way to a glowing cigarette. At 1.30am I heard a loud bang. The light went off. I went to sleep and slept quietly until morning, nothing else happened. At 7.30 in the morning I walked around, but saw nothing suspicious.

I put the paper aside. Wow! It was almost the same as what I had seen two weeks before, on 11 September 2002, near the No. 15 pit! The main thing was the light that came from an unknown source and reacted to a human glance, and the swinging torches that advanced when a person looked at them. I felt I had to get in touch immediately with these rangers, talk to them and ask about details. At least find out the date when they met with this phenomenon. Was it on 11 September 2002, or some other days in September? Judging by the weather, this had been a different day. I estimated the distance on the map. Pit No. 15 is located in the 11th quarter of the Laks forestry area. It is about 40km north-east of the place where the rangers of the Denezhkin Kamen reserve saw this 'light phenomenon' from their night camp.

At the bottom of the *Ecoved* I found the address of the Denezhkin Kamen administration and the telephone numbers. I rang the management office. I explained to the people there that I had seen a phenomenon similar to what their forest rangers V. Yefimov and V. Rudkovsky saw. I wanted to meet them and talk it over with them. The answer was that the rangers were in the forest doing their rounds and no one knew when they would be back.

In October/November 2002 I called the office again three times, but received the same answer: they were still in the forest, and no one could say when they would be back. So, at that time, my attempt to meet and talk to them failed.

With time, my interest regarding the matter faded. Not that I had forgotten about what had happened, it was just because the everyday routine of work had moved it to the far corner of my mind. Also, I did not think of it as anything significant.

I never thought that I would, at some point, get back to the events of that night. Over three years passed. On 9 January 2006, close to midnight, I was at home watching TV. I pushed the buttons on the TV remote control searching for an interesting programme. My attention was drawn to a programme called *A Mystical Hike* on one of the local TV channels. I saw just the last ten minutes of it. However, I had time to understand that it was a story of the Dyatlov tourist group who perished in February 1959 in the north of the Sverdlovsk Oblast in mysterious circumstances: nine tourists in great haste had left their tent near Mount Kholat Syakhl, with almost no clothes, almost barefoot – and froze, all of them. It came to me that the place was close to where I had been working in the mine. What was it that made the tourists leave the tent in such a hurry?

Maybe they met with the same phenomenon that I saw near the No. 15 pit in the vicinity of Ivdel, and which the rangers in the Denezhkin Kamen reserve also saw in

September 2002? Maybe this had been the cause of their death? I remembered that once I came across some publications in the press relating to details of the deaths of the nine members of Dyatlov's group who were tourists from UPI. Also a long time ago I once came across a book in which the characters were copied from the dead Dyatlov students. The information about the incident was extremely scanty. All the information I came across regarding the deaths seemed to consist more of rumours than fact. Somewhere, someone had heard or read about it. I began to search in the libraries for as much information as possible about the tourist group in the north of the Sverdlovsk Oblast. I wanted to then try and compare what the nature reserve rangers and myself had seen in September 2002 with the tragic incident that befell Dyatlov's group in February 1959. Could it be that we had met with the same phenomenon that killed the ski hikers? I decided I must meet the rangers V. Yefimov and V. Rudkovsky, as they would have more detailed and extensive information than what was described in a brief article in *Ecoved*.

I spent several days in libraries searching for materials or any publications on the Dyatlov group deaths, or anything related to the subject. In the technical library of the SevUralBauxiteRuda (SUBR) JSC they told me that they had heard and read about the Dyatlov tragedy in 1959, but no materials were available in the library. The library of V. Cheryomukhovo had nothing on the subject either.

At the Central City Library I searched the card index, but again, in vain. All the librarians had heard something about the incident, but material about the mysterious tragedy could not be found. I was advised to contact the City Library branch located in the House of Culture known as 'Sovremennik'. There was a telephone number. It was my last hope to find any material on the subject in our district. If I failed there, I would have to contact the UPI tourist club, who I was sure would tell me where to find materials on the Dyatlov group deaths.

Irina Akinshina, a librarian at the 'Sovremennik', found a few newspapers and magazines with information about the tragedy. I am very thankful to her for that. I picked most of the information from the magazine *Ural* No. 12 for 2000 and No. 1 for 2001, from the story 'The Dyatlov Pass', by Anna Matveyeva. Here I learned all about the tragic event.

Simultaneously, while searching for materials about the Dyatlov group, I was trying to locate the rangers Yefimov and Rudkovsky. These were the two who were mentioned in the newspaper *Ecoved* in September 2002 and who had witnessed an unusual light phenomenon. I wanted to hear more details from them. Could it be that such a light phenomenon was the prime cause of the Dyatlov group deaths?

I was lucky to get the director of the nature reserve on the phone. I introduced myself and explained to her the situation and why I wanted to meet the rangers. She answered that Yefimov had quit the job quite a long time ago, and Rudkovsky was again in the forest in the reserve. She was unable to give me Rudkovsky's home address and said, 'You would be better to apply to UFOlogists on that issue. Yefimov is an expert in alien worlds and the newspaper note is most likely his story.'

I sensed that she was not very convinced about such matters as strange light phenomena. It was understandable. Why should she be bothered with any mystical and strange events?

I asked her where I could find Yefimov. Her response was, 'He is from other parts. I don't know where he lives and works at present.'

I learned from other workers at the nature reserve that Yefimov was probably for some time employed at the Nordwood logging company. I visited their office only to learn that no one knew V. Yefimov and that no such person had ever worked there. It was proving to be a hard job to find him. I thought about putting an ad in a newspaper, but he might have left the district altogether.

I still hoped to meet Rudkovsky. The world is not without the good people. And good people gave me his address in the third severny settlement. I went to the settlement, found the flat where he lived and knocked at the door. A lean but strong old man with a bushy beard opened the door. It was him, Valentin Rudkovsky. I introduced myself and in some confusion explained the aim of my visit, that I had seen a light phenomenon similar to the one he saw in September 2002. I wanted to hear his story in more detail, I said. This was not just curiosity, but rather an opportunity to understand and explain the death of the people in 1959. I also told him about my attempts to find him back in 2002 after the short publication in the *Ecoved*.

He met me with interest and was very kind. We had a long talk that night. He was over 60 then. For many years he had worked as a drilling foreman in a geological survey party and when the company closed, he was offered a position as a State Inspector (Forest Ranger) in the Denezhkin Kamen nature reserve. It was just the job for him: he liked the forest and felt that in the Taiga he was in his element.

He showed me the nature reserve maps. He even found his observations diary for August 2002. Rangers keep such diaries, where they enter their daily observations of weather, reserve patrolling routes, state of the forest, animal and bird life, and generally everything they see and note on their way. Valentin told me the story of the night spent in the No. 357 forest quarter in every detail. The quarter was located north-west of Mount Denezhkin Kamen (1,492m). It was then that I learned that he was alone on that night, without V. Yefimov. And the story he told me had happened not in September but in August 2002. I asked his permission to put down his story. Here is what I got in the end, looking more like a formal account of the event:

I, Rudkovsky, Valentin Stepanovich, a State Inspector of the Denezhkin Kamen Nature Reserve, have on 29 August 2002 become witness to an unusual phenomenon in the following circumstances: I was on my way back from the Yelovsky Ouval, where I made my records, to the Solva tract, and not far from the quarter pole in quarter 357 had to stop for the night in the woods. I was alone and I made a fire about 70m from the quarter pole 357–343. I made tea but had not yet eaten. Suddenly, at 2200hrs, I saw a beam of strong light. The impression was of a neon or halogen floodlight. It pierced the forest to a depth of about a kilometre. The source of light was at some height above the ground, which I could not define, and shone at a distance of 150–200m from me in the west–east direction.

I started looking in the eastern direction, when suddenly, from that side, I saw two swinging spotlights appear, the impression was of people moving extremely fast in my direction as I stood looking at them. I thought someone was joking, or wanted to scare me and get near my fire. I dressed quickly and decided to scare them myself. I put on my boots, grabbed the gun and went to meet them. I walked about 20m, then lay behind a fallen tree trunk and looked in the direction of the spotlights. They rushed very fast in my direction exactly at the moment I looked at them.

All was quiet. Not a single sound could be heard. I raised myself from behind the tree trunk. The spotlights were approximately 50–70m away from me, but they were no longer two, but seven or eight now. They dazzled me. Immediately I lay on the ground behind the tree trunk and turned away from the spotlights. Whenever I raised my head to look at them, they would again shine on me, and dazzle me while approaching. So I spent about one and a half hours lying on the ground behind the tree trunk. I did not look at the source of light. I realised at that time that I had met something unusual, and that those had not been people but something else that could not be explained. All was quiet as before, no strange sounds.

I noted that the spotlights reacted to my eye only and decided to check whether it was true. I struck a match and lit a cigarette – no reaction. Then, in one and a half hours, I saw that the spotlights had moved and were now shining on me not from the east but from the north, still at a distance of 50–70m from me. The distance between the spotlights and the main source of light was approximately 100m. I went near my fire trying not to look, either at the source or at the spotlights. The fire was already down, I threw in more firewood, warmed my meal and ate. And then I saw that there was another beam of light from the source, now going not in the east–west but in the north–south direction as well, that is the one and the same source was now emitting beams of strong light, like that of floodlights, in two directions at approximately 90°. The light illuminated every blade of grass, the trees threw no shade. I was not looking at the source of light. I lit a cigarette and smoked, sitting with my back against a cedar tree. In all the time the light was there I made no sounds and did not shoot.

At 2.30 a.m. I heard a snapping sound as if from an electric discharge and the light was gone. Then I felt a strong gust of wind which lasted some two to three minutes. Then all was quiet again. I spent the rest of the night near the fire. In the morning I went around the place where I saw the source of light and spotlights, but noted nothing unusual or suspicious.

The next day I went near to the village of Solva. I described the unusual phenomenon I had seen to my colleagues, V.M. Yefimov and A.N. Degtyarev. A former worker of the

Denezhkin Kamen nature reserve, Ye Karpusheva, asked me in detail about this unusual phenomenon.

Soon after that, a description of this event appeared in the September 2002 issue of *Ecoved*.

I hereby certify as true the above, as recorded from my words.

Valentin seemed anxious after recalling this event. He made a sketch of the forest quarters, the position of the light source, the movement and trajectory of the spotlights and where he lay for one and a half hours behind a tree trunk.

I saw that these memories and the story had an effect on him. I asked him some questions and he responded as follows:

– Will you show me the place where you spent the night and saw the light?

– *Sure I will if you want. Although the Mansi advised me not to go there anymore.*

– Who else might have seen such a phenomenon at that time?

– *I was alone there. The next day I went to Solva and told V. Yefimov about it, and later to V. Borodyuk, and also to the senior ranger A.N. Degtyarev.*

– Where can I find them, to have a talk on the issue?

– *Degtyarev has now left the nature reserve, he now lives somewhere in Cheryomukhovo; V. Borodyuk now lives near the Kalya* [a river in Karelia, in the north-west of European Russia], *he has a house there, but I don't know his exact address. Yefimov lived for some time in Severouralsk. It is two years now since he had left the job at the nature reserve. I have heard nothing of him since then. If you happen to see them, give my regards.*

It was time to say goodbye. Valentin gave me the nature reserve quarters map so I could easily take my bearings and find quarter No. 357. We agreed to meet some time after and continue our talk. I took a picture of my hospitable friend and promised to bring him the photo. I needed some time to think over the information I had received from him.

I had absolutely no doubt that what he had seen was the same light phenomenon. There was almost a complete similarity in what he saw on 29 August 2002 and what I saw on 11 September 2002, except for a couple of conflicting details in the initial information picked from the newspaper. In *Ecoved* newspaper it was said that two rangers, V. Yefimov and V. Rudkovsky, were in the woods on that night, but then it turns out that only Rudkovsky was there. Why? The dates of the night in quarter 357 were also different: in September according to the newspaper and on 29 August 2002 as asserted by Rudkovsky. Certainly I asked Valentin about this, but he could not give a definite answer why, as so much time had passed. There was some confusion, loss of information. As he explained: 'Girls from the Denezhkin Kamen office asked me to tell them about it. In fact that was almost a month after the event. I gave some superficial explanation, and that was all. The article in the paper appeared later.'

I needed to look into this conflict between the newspaper information and the story told by Rudkovsky. If I had met him immediately in 2002, it might have been easier, while the trail was still hot. But now, more than three years later, the task was getting more complicated.

I had to know the exact date of Rudkovsky's night in quarter 357. This could be established by the observation diaries of Rudkovsky and Yefimov for September 2002. I wondered whether they had noted the fact of a night camp in quarter 357, and if the diaries still existed at all.

Again, I called the nature reserve director, Anna Kvashnina. I told her about my meeting with Rudkovsky and asked her to clarify the date of the event. I also asked her if I could see Rudkovsky's diary for September 2002. Her answer was that the diaries were kept in the archives in the office in Vsevolozhsk. She said: 'Nobody is going to search for anything for you. Get in touch with the worker for the nature reserve, Galina Neustroyeva, and go along and see for yourself.'

What an opportunity ... to get hold of the observation diaries for September 2002! I decided to go to Vsevolozhsk immediately.

Galina Neustroyeva, a lab assistant, advised me on the telephone how to find the nature reserve office in Vsevolozhsk. We agreed that I would catch the first bus there, and she would find the rangers' diaries for me.

I wanted to make sure from the diaries that V. Rudkovsky met with the 'light set' on 29 August 2002 and not in September 2002, as the account in *Ecoved* newspaper asserted.

It was the end of January 2006, biting frost, minus 30°C with a strong wind. As I waited at a bus stop I was frozen to the bone, despite my sheepskin coat and felt boots. Just then I thought of the members of the Dyatlov group on the side of Mount Kholat Syakhl open to winds, on that night of 1/2 February 1959, when they were left without their warm clothes, shoes, hats, mittens, far from warm houses, and without hope of help from anywhere. How long could they stand that? What was it that made them leave the tent so hastily, without clothes, without an opportunity to get back?

I found the office in Vsevolozhsk in a small house in Plaksina Street. Galina brought the observation diaries of rangers Rudkovsky and Yefimov for September 2002. I sat down and started reading. On the nature reserve map I traced their routes in every forest quarter in September. Neither Rudkovsky nor Yefimov had been to the Yelovsky Ouval in September 2002. I looked at the date: 11 September

2002, exactly the day I watched the 'light phenomenon' in the Ivdel district near the No. 15 pit.

Here is the record made by V. Rudkovsky, dated 11 September 2002:

t + 6 °C Small rain
r. Solva – r. Kriv
Quarter 439 – woodcock
Quarter 455 – grouse
Quarter 499 – grey hen took wing
Quarter 499 – bear's marks

The weather on that day was the same as in the Ivdel district near the No. 15 pit, but on that day V. Rudkovsky was too far away from quarter 357. Also, in Rudkovsky's diary for September 2002, there was no mention of a night camp in the woods. I remembered Valentin mentioning that it was his habit to make a note of every night he spent in the woods in his diaries. The September 2002 inspection routes of Rudkovsky and Yefimov were also different. Clearly, Rudkovsky's observation of the 'light phenomenon' had occurred – but on 29 August 2002, not in September. He was also alone.

The date was now clear. I said goodbye to Galina and caught the next bus from Vsevolozhsk. It was now important to locate and talk to the people who met Rudkovsky after his encounter with the 'light phenomenon'. They may add or at least clarify certain things. After some time I was lucky to find former nature reserve workers who were mentioned by Rudkovsky: A. Degtyarev in Cheryomukhovo, V. Borodyuk on the Kalya, and even V. Yefimov in Severouralsk. I talked with Degtyarev over the telephone, and personally met with the other two. All of them remembered Rudkovsky's story of the 'light phenomenon' reacting to a human glance, which he had seen on the night he spent in quarter 357. All of them talked of Valentin as a knowledgeable forest ranger and a good and honest person whose words could be trusted. I gave them regards from him.

I asked Yefimov why his name was mentioned as a witness of the 'light phenomenon' in the *Ecoved* story, despite the fact that he had not been there at that time. He said: 'You see, it might be that the nature reserve management gave one errand for two to perform. To make it quicker we might separate. I think this was the case that time. That is how my name got in the story, by a mere chance. Despite that, I wasn't with him that night. Rudkovsky was alone.'

Okay, so another discrepancy was cleared up. I was told: 'Well, well, you were really lucky to make Valentin talk about that case. He has never been too talkative.' I replied: 'Oh, you see this is probably because we had both had the same experience, only at different times and places, we had plenty to talk about.'

So, what had happened to the nine skiers on 1 February 1959? I tried to look at the situation, bearing in mind the results of the investigation of the Dyatlov case and the group's diaries, and to reconstruct the tragedy in the context of the 'light phenomenon' observations of 29 August 2002 and 11 September 2002. What follows is how I see the events that led to a tragedy on the eastern slope of Mount Kholat Syakh.

On the fifth day of the ski trip the group decided to make camp for the night in a tent on the eastern slope of Mount Kholat Syakhl. Most probably, they wanted to start for Mount Otorten at dawn the next day.

With a view to using the remaining daylight, approximately at 5 p.m. they set up the tent with the entrance looking south, and stacked backpacks and other things inside. Someone of the group took the last photo as the tent was being set up. With them they had food for two to three days, an axe, a saw, a small camp stove that could be suspended inside the tent. The stove was filled with firewood they had brought along from the previous camp. The edge of the forest was some 1.5km away from the tent, and there was no other place to take firewood from.

The temperature was getting lower towards nightfall and a strong wind blew. According to the investigation data, the air temperature in the region on that day was minus 25–30°C, with a strong wind. A campfire and cooking a hot dinner in the open was out of the question. They did not have enough firewood for that, and the strong wind would prevent it.

Most probably Thibeaux-Brignolle, or Tibo as friends called him, was 'on duty' that night. The rest took their places in the tent. They took off their outer garments, footwear and hats and lay trying to make themselves warm with their breath, under blankets and their outerwear. They had no sleeping bags, just blankets. There was not much space inside the tent, so all, except for the one on duty, either sat or lay in their places.

Each member of the group in turn made records in the group diary of the trip, additionally some of them kept personal diaries, but on that night not a single entry was made. They probably planned to do so after the stove was fired and it got warmer in the tent. They were preparing for a snack: brisket was sliced, and crackers were taken out. There was some coffee in flasks left from the last camp.

Tibo, as the man on duty, stayed with his outerwear and boots on. After 6 p.m., already in almost complete darkness, Tibo leaves the tent with a flashlight 'to do a number one' and is surprised to see a white swinging light probably coming in the south–north direction. Like from a projector, the beam hits the slope of the mountain where the tent stands. Tibo cries to the others in the tent that he sees something very unusual. Being a realist and a materialist (and just out of curiosity) he wants to have a closer look to understand what this might be. He even points his flashlight in the direction of the light source. At this instance the source of light reacts to his glance, changes the direction of the beam and floods Tibo and the tent with bright white light. Immediately a few torches, or projectors, separate from the source. They swing and approach, catch his glance, and while Tibo continues to look in amazement, an approaching torch sends a strong pointed shock-wave pulse with a bright light flash aimed at the man's glance. Involuntarily, Tibo turns his face away to the left from the dazzling flash of light, and the pointed shock wave hits him in the temple, he sustains the 'fracture of the rh temporal bone'. He cries in pain and falls unconscious. He lets go of the flashlight, which lands on the tent roof (later rescuers will find this flashlight lying there).

Zolotarev and Dubinina rush to him from the tent. They bend over their friend lying on the ground and try to pull him to the tent entrance. Zolotarev is in front, Dubinina is behind. They hold Tibo and from their bent position look at the swinging torches, searching for a human glance. Maybe they see something even more horrible and inexplicable. They also get a blow of a pointed shock wave, which was probably aimed at their glance, but due to their abruptly raised heads and change of position, they receive a blow in the ribs. Zolotarev sustains 'five broken ribs on the right side on the breast and mid-axillary line, with haemorrhage into axillary muscle'. He was in a bent position, with his right side exposed to the light and shock-wave source.

Dubinina has 'four broken ribs at left on the mid-clavicular and mid-axillary line and six ribs at right on the mid-clavicular line', i.e. she looks behind her at the source of light and shock wave and she gets a blow in her back. This causes her tongue to tear off.

If they were standing still at the moment of the shock-wave pulse, the blow would have hit their glance, their eyes. All three received very serious wounds, but two of them had nevertheless retained an ability to move for some time. According to the autopsy, such injuries could not have been inflicted either by a stone or a fall on stones, since the skin and the soft tissues remained undamaged. The above injuries are very much like an injury from an air-shock wave.

The possibility is not excluded that those three were not just badly injured by a shock wave, but also dazzled by a bright flash of light coming from the swinging torches or from the source of light and preceding the shock wave. Involuntarily, they reacted to this bright painful flash of light and changed their body position. In a brief moment they were hit by a pointed shock wave.

Thibeaux-Brignolle was unconscious, but he could have still shown signs of life for two to three hours. Dubinina might have lived ten to twenty minutes after being injured. She might have stayed conscious. Zolotarev, being less injured, might have lived longer. In the heat of the moment, both Dubinina and Zolotarev could have continued moving by themselves. The other six tourists, already preparing to sleep in their places in the tent, get alarmed. The light appearing from nowhere and penetrating into the tent through the curtain, the groans of their friends crying that they have been wounded by light torches … Maybe it was something even more terrible and aggressive that they saw near the tent.

It may be that, besides the blast wave, as these torches got nearer they emitted a narrow-focused infrasonic beam of energy (pulse), which acted physically on the tourists, inflicting mortal wounds and psychologically affecting the other six in the tent.

'The human hearing capacity lies in the range from 16 to 20,000Hz. Sounds above or below this range act on the human body. Infrasound in the range of 7–8Hz is the most dangerous for humans. It is the frequency at which many human internal organs oscillate; 7Hz is the average frequency of brain alpha-rhythms. A sufficiently high infrasound amplitude (volume) may be the cause of rupture of vital organs, epileptic seizures, bouts of panic' (magazine *Kaleidoscope*, No. 28, 10 July 2006). Could it be that Luda Dubinina lost her tongue due to the effect of infrasound? The others in the tent were also affected by infrasound but to a lesser degree. They were not injured but the infrasound made them panic.

Panic breaks out in the tent. Where to run from these lights, those swinging and killing projector-torches? There is no escape through the tent entrance! The escape is blocked by the raging light!

Someone cuts the tent wall from inside, they rush out, having no time to put on their outerwear. They don't know yet that they must just turn away from the light, not to look at the torches, and then, in a minute or two, those killing torches would move away and leave them alone. But they did not and could not know that.

It was enough for just one of them to keep looking at the swinging torches for the light to stay near. The territory around the tent was flooded with the white flouncing light. It made them run, without their clothes on, away from the tent, away from that terrible place. Were they panic-stricken? I think yes. That period of contact with an unknown 'light force' and the action of infrasound inside and outside the tent was the period of utter panic. This is only natural, given the extreme situation they were in. This is confirmed by the fact they had run so far away from the tent without warm clothes, which was a sure way to death on the cold and windy winter night.

A similar view regarding the start of the tragedy was expressed by Alexsey Koskin, a tourist who had visited the

Dyatlov Pass. In a letter to the editor of a Moscow newspaper he expressed the view that the members of the group were alerted by something outside the tent and the first three who went outside were confronted by something dangerous, which I believe was the shock wave.

I believe the skiers tried to pull themselves together, they took Tibo who was unconscious and, helping the other wounded, started moving away from the tent in an organised way, down the slope. The half-dressed tourists were moving down, towards the edge of the forest, not in the direction of their storage shed by following their own previous day's ski track, but further north. Why? Simply because in the direction they had come from by day there was now the source of light, and danger. They could not have moved in that direction. Willingly or unwillingly, someone would look back at the light, and the light responded to their glance and pointed its beams at them, and this made them move further and further, down the slope and away from the tent.

One of the skiers who was the last in the line followed the track made by the others, carrying unconscious Tibo on his back. Luda Dubinina, badly wounded, was moving with someone's help, then she was also carried. Wounded Zolotarev moved by himself.

Twenty-five days later, the rescue party found the tent and human tracks of pressed snow, the 'columns' of foot-prints leading 500m away from the tent. The February winds blew loose snow from the mountain slope, leaving only the snow 'columns' of human footprints. A path made in snow by human feet keeps until all the snow thaws away. Virgin snow near the path gets blown away or sets down from the warm air in spring, while the pressed snow col-umns stay longer and would be the last ones to thaw. So the skiers left this 500m long track of pressed snow 'columns'.

The snow near the 'columns' was gone with the wind so, when found by the rescue party on 26 February 1959, the tracks rose above the coat of snow. Two, or maybe three, wounded tourists were dragged over the snow. The closer to the forest, the deeper became the snow.

Sinking in 2m deep snow, with tremendous effort the tourists carrying their wounded stopped at the edge of the forest near a cedar standing on its own. Judging by the tracks, they covered this almost 2km distance in about one and a half to two hours.

The wind was still very strong near the cedar, so the wounded were carried 70m further down, near the frozen stream. The snow was very deep there, but the wind was not so strong. There, the beams of light did not follow them, and they did not see the light any more, since it stayed higher up on the mountain, near the tent.

The tourists cut spruce branches for the wounded and started making a hole in deep snow to hide them from wind and frost. Already all the members of the Dyatlov group had their feet, hands and faces frostbitten. On the cold, windy night they were left without outer garments, mittens and caps. The tourists realised that without warm garments they would not live until morning and would surely freeze. What to do in such a situation? It might be good to make a big fire to get warm until morning. Why did they not do that? Most probably, they abstained from making a big fire for fear of attracting the lights, to avoid a repetition of the horror they had felt near the tent. They probably supposed that the light of a candle in the tent, a burning match or a flashlight had provoked the aggressive action of that unknown light force against them. They did not know that the 'light set' did not react to the light of a campfire, or an electric torch, or noise. It only responded to a human glance.

They could not move deeper into the forest either, because they had not the strength to carry the wounded across that deep snow and could not leave them alone. They also understood that they should not go too far from the tent, because their clothes and skis were there and they would need them to get out of the Taiga to civilisation.

It is tens of kilometres to any inhabited places. They could only rely on themselves. They dug a hole in deep snow near the frozen stream and hid their wounded from the wind and cold. Kolevatov stayed with his wounded companions, who were probably already dead from mortal wounds. His foot is dislocated, bandaged with a piece of cloth. The remaining five go 50–70m to the stand-alone cedar. They understand that they need to get back to the tent. Once there, they would collect the tent, the stove and clothes and bring them on skis down to the wounded. They would then make the wounded warm and get warm themselves.

But the flouncing light that has wounded their friends is still there, near the tent. Rustem Slobodin climbs up the cedar to see the tent. Breaking the lower dry branches with his frostbitten hands, and leaving pieces of skin from his palms, he climbs up the cedar to a height of 5m. He can see from this height the tent flooded with the light, but the cedar branches close the view. He breaks branches to make an opening for a better view. The branches, though thick, give way easily in the frost (cedar is a generally fragile tree). Slobodin sees that the dancing light is still there, near the tent. He feels very cold up the tree, but continues watching. At approximately 10.30 p.m. the skiers hear a strong snapping sound as of an electric discharge. Slobodin cries from the cedar that the light near the tent is gone, and that means the way to the tent is open (Ranger Rudkovsky reported hearing a similar sound before the light was gone on 29 August 2002). At this moment, a squally wind rises and blows Slobodin from the cedar. Falling, he tries to grab branches with his frostbitten hands, but they break under his weight. He falls down and hits his head on the tree trunk or protruding roots. Slobodin was found with an injury: 'cranial vault fracture 6cm long, with a parting up to 0.1cm'. In the heat of the moment Slobodin pays no attention to his bad wound and wants to crawl to the tent. In two to three minutes the squally wind dies down.

After that, Igor Dyatlov decides to make a small fire from cedar branches to serve as a light landmark for those crawling across the snow to the tent. Two of them, Doroshenko and Krivonischenko, stay to support the fire, while Dyatlov, Slobodin and Zina Kolmogorova make for the tent. It is a hard job to make their way up the slope in deep snow. It is like pulling up your body from a boggy marsh at every step.

Why did they not use their old trail to get to the tent? It may be that the blizzard had swept all traces, and they feared to take the wrong direction in the dark and fail to find the tent. Or probably they decided that they would reach the tent quicker moving in a straight line, with the fire acting as a landmark behind them.

Desperately, with their last strength, the three half-dressed frostbitten tourists try to make their way to the tent across deep snow. Their palms and feet get numb and stiff. The tormenting pain of frostbite rises higher and higher in the body. Their bodies tremble from hypothermia and cramps. There is no way to escape the cold and the biting wind. To get warm they try to crawl faster across the snow. But they quickly lose strength and breath. The last bits of strength and warmth are lost. They get sleepy. Their life forces are exhausted. They freeze.

George Krivonischenko and Yury Doroshenko supported the fire as long as they could, it kept on for one and a half to two hours, but it could not make them warm. They put their frostbitten feet and hands into the fire but did not feel the pain. They froze. Rescuers found them near the cedar tree with burnt hands and feet.

By midnight, only Kolevatov was still alive. He had been given the task to stay in the depression near the stream close to the wounded Thibeaux-Brignolle and Luda Dubinina, and to wait for the others to come back with the tent and clothes.

Kolevatov goes up to the cedar, finds Krivonischenko and Doroshenko dead, cuts their clothes off with a knife and brings the clothes to the wounded. The clothes cut and taken off Doroshenko and Krivonischenko were later found on the dead body of mortally wounded Luda Dubinina. Would she still have been alive then? Hardly probable. Kolevatov could not believe that she was dead and tried to make her life last as long as he could, and could not leave her. So he froze near her, waiting in vain for his friends to come back with the tent and warm things. Cold death has taken him too. At about 2 a.m. it was all over. The blizzard was covering over with snow the dead, cold bodies of the nine tourists.

My description of what had happened to the Dyatlov group from the moment of setting up the tent on the slope of Mount Kholat Syakhl to the death of the last of the tourists is not yet an established fact. This is my own version of the incident or, if you like, a new version of the tragedy. It is based on the diary records of the tourists, the materials of the investigation, and the facts I personally met with on 11 September 2002 in the Ivdel district, and what V. Rudkovsky saw on 29 August 2002 in the Denezhkin Kamen nature reserve. One should not try to find a logical explanation of the developments of this tragedy.

Why had the skiers acted so? Why had they moved in that direction and not in the other? Many of their actions on 1 February 1959 seem wrong and illogical to us. But they were without clothes, and they all froze. They were in an extreme situation, and could not have acted otherwise. No one knew what to do in that situation, in the presence of that 'light set'. They all fought for their lives desperately to the end.

The main mystery is the fact that the whole of the group left the tent. One of the members of the rescue party, V. Karelin, who had known them all well, wrote: 'The people in the Dyatlov group were such that they could have become scared only by something extraordinary, something that was out of the ordinary course of things.'

I think that it was the 'light set' that appeared with the fall of the night on the eastern slope of the Ural Mountains, reacting to a human glance by sending swinging torches and an infrasonic shock wave, which caused the tourists to leave the tent and finally killed the whole of the group.

Should any one of the Dyatlov group have remained alive to tell about the 'light set', the story would probably have been interpreted by the authorities at the time as the 'machinations of imperialists' and they would not have acknowledged what actually happened, since it was outside the official 'materialistic' view of the world. Investigator Ivanov had his own opinion, which did not fit in the framework of materialism. However, we must also thank the authorities. Huge material resources were involved in the search for the lost tourists, involving transport and aviation, also helicopters (which were quite rare in the 1950s). Not many lost tourists and alpinists would have received so much attention. Rescue teams, hunters, the military and investigators all took part in the search. In that deserted place, under severe winter conditions of the north Urals they performed a huge amount of work. The information gathered by these people will someday allow the cause of the Dyatlov group's deaths to be found out.

What did the official authorities do after the tragedy? They made the relatives sign a non-disclosure declaration; they wanted the dead to be buried in Ivdel, not in Sverdlovsk; they closed access to the area for tourists for three years.

This caused multiple rumours about tests of some secret weapon in the area, and that the true information was being concealed from the people. But what to conceal? No one really knows what happened. Yet the causes of the tragedy need to be discussed, for the simple reason to suppress futile attacks on cosmonautics and intelligence services.

What might a 'light set' be doing in the No. 15 pit? Why did it set light on the waste rock dump? The pit hides nothing secret, just common manufactured mining machines, general mining technology and the dump, which is a pile of limestone mixed with clay. If intelligence services needed such information, they could easily get it in daytime, without the need for a light show. And what were they looking for in the dense forest beyond Mount Denezhkin Kamen, where ranger V. Rudkovsky had watched this phenomenon?

Most probably, this one and the same 'light set' makes its appearance in different parts east of the Ural Ridge following some programme built into it by no one knows who and no one knows when. It may be doing ground surveys at definite locations by picking information with a light beam.

Here are the approximate co-ordinates of its appearance:

– 29 August 2002: 60°30" N 59°25" E, from 10 p.m. to 2.30 a.m. Observed by V. Rudkovsky in quarter 357 of the Denezhkin Kamen nature reserve.

– 11 September 2002: 60°40" N 60°15" E, at 11 p.m. in quarter 11 of the Laksa forestry. The 'set' stayed there approximately from 9.30 p.m. to 2 a.m.

– 1 February 1959: 61°45" N 59°20" E. The eastern slope of Mount Kholat Syakhl. Time approximately from 6 p.m. to 10.30 p.m.

According to Rudkovsky, the light appeared shortly before it got dark. Probably, the 'light set' starts its survey after dark and continues at certain points of the earth for four to four and a half hours. Rudkovsky claimed that at 2.30 a.m. he heard a loud snapping sound, like from a strong electric discharge, and then the light was gone. After that, for two to three minutes, a strong squally wind rose.

We may suppose that on 11 September 2002, the 'set' started working in No. 15 pit after dark, i.e. at 9.30 p.m., and finished at 2 a.m.

On 1 February 1959, on Mount Kholat Syakhl, the light the tourists saw appeared at 6 p.m. and went out at 10.30 p.m. or around this time (plus or minus thirty minutes).

Could space satellites have recorded this light on 29 August 2002 and 11 September 2002? It might be possible to clarify the time of operation of the 'light set' by this data. Or maybe there are records of similar light effects in other places?

I always find it difficult remembering the event of having seen the 'light set', the more so every time I have to prove to someone that this had really happened to me. I try not to think about this as some awful experience. It was probably for this reason that I put this subject aside in 2002. Rudkovsky had a similar reaction, as he told me himself. Rudkovsky's former friend in the nature reserve, V. Yefimov, told me that when he met Valentin after the night spent in the woods near that 'light set', Valentin looked a bit 'haywire' and sluggish, especially the first day after it had happened. Then, gradually, he began to feel better. After August 2002 Valentin was seriously ill twice, although nothing of the kind had ever happened to him before. In 2004 he underwent serious surgery. After the meeting with the 'light set' I myself had two serious injuries in the Ivdel district. I would not link my injuries directly with what I saw on 11 September 2002. But still, these are issues to be considered.

After I read the material of the Dyatlov case investigation, it dawned on me that we, Rudkovsky and myself, had got off easily. We could have gone mad or received a due portion of a shock wave from the 'light set'. We were lucky, just because of having grasped in a short while that the 'set' responded to our glance and that one should plainly look away from the source of light and the approaching torches. For a group, this may have been impossible to have been quickly understood.

Science moves forward. In the flow of information we may sometimes oversee serious scientific discoveries that have been made in recent times. Under the guidance of scientists, a new, fifth, state of matter was obtained at an orbital station in outer space: frozen plasma. Before that, mankind knew of only four states of matter: solid, gaseous, liquid and plasma. Here is the discovery of one more: the frozen plasma state. It opens up great opportunities in power engineering and prospects for building spacecraft capable of reaching other planets and stars. New super-heavy elements appear in the Mendeleev periodic table. When stores of oil and gas come to an end on the Earth these elements will allow power to be safely generated from them. Also amazing scientific research results have been obtained in the USA and Russia: 'graphic thought record' ('*myslegraphia*' in Russian) – an imprint of a human thought may appear on photographic film. In other words, thought may be photographed. There was an article about such effect in *Komsomolskaya Pravda* in April 2006.

Could the 'light set' be equipped with an instrument able to catch human thought via a glance? When the person looks away, the 'set' loses sight of the person and leaves him or her alone. Or possibly does not lose sight of the person, but processes human thought according to some internal program and determines whether such a 'witness' needs to be eliminated. This smells of something extraterrestrial.

The fact that the 'light set' may not just amaze people with its abnormal behaviour (its main feature is response to human glance), but also be aggressive and inflict mortal injuries to people with a fine-focused shock wave and make them panic had caused me to sit down to commit to paper my version of the Ivdel incident.

According to my version, such were the injuries received on 1 February 1959 by the skiers: Thibeaux-Brignolle, Zolotarev and Luda Dubinina. This made the half-dressed tourists leave the tent and run as fast as they could, and finally killed them all.

This is an extremely rare phenomenon. But people must work out and remember certain rules of safe behaviour when meeting with such an effect, in order to avoid a repetition of the Dyatlov incident.

First, one has to simply turn away and not look at the source of light. One should leave the place as fast as possible. I think if someone happens to observe the phenomenon and they have a camera with them, they should take a photo only while looking away, or with closed eyes and in a very short period of time. Such occasional encounters of people with the 'light set' will surely happen in the future. I am sure there have already been many. When something ends well, people make little of it (so it happened to me after I met with the 'light phenomenon' on 11 September 2002). Other meetings end in tragedy, leaving silent dead bodies behind and many questions with no answers.

For example, in summer 2004, in the Taiga near Severouralsk, an experienced hunter left his hut without his outer clothes and never came back. Later, his body was found without signs of violent death (reported in the newspaper *Nashe Slovo* dated 27 February 2006). I got interested in the mysterious death of this person and decided to look for details of the case.

This is what I learned from relatives of the deceased. Sergey Baryshnikov, 50 years old, a physically strong person, a miner from the city of Severouralsk, knew the Taiga very well. He used his vacation time for professional hunting. He had a hut somewhere on the River Molmys in the Perm Oblast, beyond the Ural Ridge, where he lived and hunted. On 14 August 2004, he left Severouralsk in his car to check whortleberry fields on the Yelovaya Griva (Spruce Mane) ridge. This is a place on the road to Kvarkusha. He took no gun and planned to be back home on the same day. There were two dogs with him: 3-year-old Belka and 3-month-old Buran.

He drove from Severouralsk via Bayanovka to the west, in the direction of Mount Teremki on the Yelovvaya ridge, 60km from Severouralsk. There, 1km from the main road, he left his car. He did not come back, neither on that night, nor on the next day.

His relatives and friends started a search. The car was soon found because they knew where he was headed for, but there was no sign of him. A rescue team from Karpinsk was invited twice, because Severouralsk had no such team at that time. People from the Severouralsk Bauxite mines (SUBR) and other city organisations were involved in the search. A sniffer dog was brought but it failed to find a trail, because of too many footprints near the car.

Within a few days, his dogs Buran and Belka were found. The Mansi said that if the dogs had left their master it must mean he is dead. The search lasted two weeks. On 3 September 2004, in the vicinity of Mount Sredny Sennoi

Kamen, a cedar nuts procurement team found his dead body approximately 20km from where he had left his car. He was without footwear and half-dressed. He wore only a singlet and sports pants. There were no traces of violent death. He had died of heart failure, which had developed as a result of strong pneumonia, which means that he died of hypothermia. His stomach was empty, despite the fact that at that time of year the Taiga abounds in cedar cones, many of which lay on the ground, and whortleberry.

What had happened to a normal healthy man in the Taiga? Being an experienced Taiga dweller and hunter he could not get lost as he knew the area very well. We can only suppose that he had met with something very extraordinary.

And here, too, we may see analogies with the deaths of the Dyatlov group. What happened to cause the hunter to suffer from hypothermia and die out in the Taiga? This is what I suppose had happened. For some reason he stopped in the Taiga for the night of 14/15 August 2004. It could be that he planned to look around the area more thoroughly. Or the dogs, Belka and Buran, sensing the infrasound emitted by the 'light set' ran away, so he went after them and was compelled to stay in the Taiga for the night. He could not leave the dogs and go home alone. (It is known that dogs and cats perceive vibrations below 20Hz, i.e. infrasound. That is why it is said of them that 'they smell trouble': animals are often the first to get alarmed and leave a village where an earthquake is soon to take place, which is preceded by infrasonic emission.)

In the evening the hunter made a fire, took off his boots and outer garments, which were wet from the rain, and started drying his clothes near the fire. Suddenly, in the dark, at approximately 10.30 p.m., he sees a strip of swinging light as if from a projector. He watches the source of light with interest. At that moment, swinging torches separate from the source of light and quickly move in his direction through the forest. In amazement, he continues looking at the torches. They get near and suddenly a strong pulse of infrasound hits him.

It may be that the blow and the shock caused fear and panic in the man. He runs away from the place half-dressed and barefoot. The dogs follow him. The impact of infrasound and the shock wave was so strong that he never recovered his normal mental condition. All his further actions were inadequate to save him.

Over a period of a number of days he wandered in the Taiga, did not pick berries or nuts, made no effort to make himself warm and find a way to habitation. He moved at random, without direction, in places where neither a house nor a road could be found. The weather was cold and rainy. He got a cold, a strong pneumonia developed, and in a few days he died, 20km from his car.

Had it been so or not, no one can tell for sure. One can only suppose. Another supposition is that he might have died from a lightning bolt.

Over 100 Russian satellites are orbiting the Earth today. There is a round-the-clock observation of the whole of the country's territory from outer space. If satellite control centres had registered luminescence in that area on the night of 14/15 August 2004, such records could serve as indirect proof to the fact of an experienced Taiga dweller being affected by a 'light set'. Can anyone take out this data of satellite observation? Do such people or organisations exist?

Here are the approximate map co-ordinates of the place where S.I. Baryshnikov could have been on that night: 60°07" N, 59°20" E. If necessary, more precise co-ordinates of the places where I and Rudkovsky saw the 'light set' in operation can be indicated on larger-scale maps, or using instruments, up to fractions of a second. If the three cases of illumination that had taken place at different times and locations were registered by satellites, much would be explained, the Dyatlov group deaths included.

The hunter's dog, Belka, had also received some stress, or probably the 'light set' infrasonic action had an effect on her. Being a cheerful and active creature, she now looked quiet, frightened, as if feeling some guilt, putting her ears down all the time. Gradually, she recovered her normal condition. She still lives with S.I. Baryshnikov's widow.

What is this trouble that wanders the Taiga at night? Who can give an answer? Maybe its appearance was noted not only in the Taiga?

I visited the Dyatlov graves at the Mikhailovskoe Cemetery in Ekaterinburg. On the 4m high monument there are nine photographs of young and beautiful boys and girls; the sign on the back of the monument reads: 'In eternal memory of tourists of Ural Polytechnic Institute tragically killed in north Urals on 2 February 1959'.

Their deaths were not in vain. The price of their deaths helps us to understand the unknown phenomenon that had killed them. By picking every grain of truth and systematising such unusual phenomena, and with the current progress in science, people will someday answer the question of what that 'light set' was like, what was the purpose of its appearance on the eastern slope of the Ural Mountains, where it came from, and who sent it to us.

9

The present

If any of the Dyatlov party were still alive in 2012, they would probably have been getting too old to make the arduous journey from Ekaterinburg to Kholat Syakhl. Luda Dubinina, for instance, who was 20 years old at the time of her death in 1959, would have been 73 years old in May 2012 had she lived. There would have been some changes on the route they took as well as changes elsewhere, not least the sweeping away of the old Soviet Union, starting with the fall of the Berlin Wall in 1989. The name of the city they started their journey from changed from Sverdlovsk to Ekaterinburg in 1991, and had they been around in 1991 and living in the newly renamed city they may have started to regularly see foreigners for the first time – until then it had been a closed city. There are a number of high-rise buildings in the city now, giving it a modern appearance and lifting it out of the Soviet era 'look', although there is still plenty of evidence of Soviet-style architecture.

The outside of the Ural Polytechnic Institute (UPI) that the Dyatlov group attended is still the same as it looked in 1959, although in 2011 it merged with the other university in Ekaterinburg, the Ural State University (URGU). Both are now known as the Ural Federal University (URFU), although many people in the city will probably still refer to it as UPI.

Anyone travelling north from Ekaterinburg on the same route as the Dyatlov group will see more or less what they saw on the journey. The main railway station in Ekaterinburg is much the same as it was in 1959 and the sombre Siberian Taiga they looked out upon is still the same. The military and nuclear facilities in the region, which were the cause of spy flights in the Cold War, are still there and are now watched by satellites. The gaseous diffusion plant for the enrichment of plutonium U-235 at Verkh Neyvinsk has been upgraded, and the huge facility for the production of (and separate facility for) storage of nuclear warheads at Nizhnyaya Tura has been expanded since 1959. A non-Russian wishing to recreate the Dyatlov group's journey from Ekaterinburg should be aware of these military and nuclear plants as they are within clearly defined restricted zones, yet the railway north and the road both travel very close to them. The first closed area to avoid is to the west from the railway line between Nizhny Tagil and Ivdel, limited by the River Ivdel from the north and by a line from Kushva-Serebryanka from the south (excluding the railway and the aforementioned towns). The second closed area is part of the Neyvansk and Kirovgrad regions, limited by a line from Verkh-Neyvinsk to Kalinov to the railway station at Murzinka to the village of Belorechka to the village of Neyvo-Rudyanka back to Verkh-Neyvinsk. Many people have probably made the journey north while being oblivious to these restrictions. If by chance someone should find themselves within these areas and they are stopped, they would need to have a very good explanation as to what they were doing there.

These facilities were joined in 1996 by a new underground nuclear command post for the Russian Strategic Rocket Forces at Kosvinsky Mountain in the Ural Mountains, west of the town of Serov. This post is intended to launch all Russian nuclear missiles in the event that the nuclear command facilities near Moscow are knocked out by a pre-emptive nuclear strike. Although this is well off the route north from Ekaterinburg to Serov and Ivdel, it is in the mountains south of where the Dyatlov group died and also should be avoided. Also in the region, but not on the direct route north, is a large ICBM base for road mobile SS-25 missiles to the east of Nizhny Tagil, with a further facility close to the south-east of Ekaterinburg named Kosulin-1 (near the village of Kosulin), used for for storage of nuclear weapons with facilities to take rail-mobile SS-25 ICBMs. In short, the eastern Urals region is a large area but packed with sensitive military nuclear facilities.

Upon reaching Ivdel itself, it could be said to still contain some descendants of 'cops and prisoners'. The Gulags have disappeared from across Russia and been replaced by far fewer prisons and camps. The approximately 100 Gulag camps and subcamps around Ivdel and the surrounding region in Stalin's time have been replaced by one particular camp that occupies a sinister place in the hierarchy of Russian prisons. Known as Maximum Security Penal Colony No FBU-IK 56 and situated 25 miles (40km) north of Ivdel (at the village of Lozvinsky) and holding around 300 inmates at any one time, it is one of five colonies in Russia in which the majority of convicts would have been sentenced to death, but are serving life terms instead after Russia's moratorium on the death penalty in 1999 (which was passed but not ratified, although death sentences have been suspended since).[1] The Ivdel special colony is nicknamed 'The Black Eagle', so named because of the sculpture of an eagle holding a serpent's head that is located at the entrance and made by one of the inmates, a former traffic policeman Khabas Zakuraev, who is jailed for murder. Zakuraev explains his sculpture as 'an eagle searches everywhere for carrion, he who breaks the law is carrion himself'.[2] Interestingly, the other four Russian colonies that are identified by numbers also have nicknames (The Black Dolphin, The Vologda Coin, The White Swan and Village Harp).[3]

One facet of the Gulags that had not changed in the years since Stalin and the Dyatlov tragedy was that an inmate attempting to escape from The Black Eagle would still run the risk of being shot by a guard from one of the perimeter watch-towers.

It would be prudent for visitors to register their presence with the Department of the Interior, Migration Registration Service (only necessary if staying overnight in a hotel) in Ivdel and state the route being taken in the northern Urals, although many people do not do this. Trucks can still be hired in Ivdel, just as the Dyatlov group did to travel north to start the journey to the pass, then continuing either on foot or with skis and skimobiles in winter. One notable difference, however, is the village of Vizhay, where the group spent the night of 25/26 January. Although relatively small, Vizhay was an established village, but it was burned down in 2010 in one of the many summer forest fires that regularly sweep though the region.

On the mountain itself (Kholat Syakhl) there is very little visible change from the night that claimed the lives of the group, with only the memorial plaque on the rock at the saddle of the mountain to show human input. It is said that the cedar tree where the bodies of Yury Doroshenko and George Krivonischenko were first found can still be identified although this is probably more wishful thinking. In keeping with what appears to be happening elsewhere in the world, the area is becoming subject to the problem of rubbish being left behind by visitors. Despite being a very remote area, there is a steady throughput of visitors, not just to the Dyatlov Pass itself but also passing through to other scenic areas of interest, such as the large rock formations known as Manpupuner, roughly 75 miles (120km) to the north-west of Kholat Syakhl.

While the story of the Dyatlov tragedy is only becoming better known in the West in recent years, the story of the deaths of the skiers is well known in Ekaterinburg and the eastern Urals region. Every once in a while, something happens that prompts further speculation in the local and Russian media. The most recent example concerns the disappearance of an aircraft from Serov airfield. It will be remembered that the Dyatlov party passed through Serov on their way north from Sverdlovsk (Ekaterinburg) on 24 January 1959 when they had trouble with the police, when George Krivonischenko started singing at the railway station there and later the group had more trouble with a drunk who accused them of stealing his wallet.

On 11 June 2012 (the eve of Russia Day) an Antonov An-2R with the registration RA-40312 belonging to a local operator Avia Zov took off illegally from Serov Airport.[4] On board were believed to be a group of twelve, who had all been having a party and drinking heavily. The group included the chief of police in Serov, three police inspectors, a Serov airport guard, a security guard for a private company at the airport, a shop owner, an unemployed man, a pensioner, plus three others including the pilot. A number of cars belonging to the group were left at the airport when the An-2R took off. The reason for the drunken party commandeering the aircraft was that they wanted to go somewhere to continue the party, to go fishing and take a sauna. From 10 p.m. on 11 June 2012 when the plane took off, there has been no further sighting of the aircraft or its party on board. It was widely assumed that the aircraft had crashed, particularly considering the drunken state of the party. However, despite the Russian Ministry of

Emergency Situations searching an area of 275,800km/sq by 20 July 2012, nothing has been found. The Siberian Taiga is vast and the aircraft may have gone into a river, lake or ravine. By the end of summer 2012, the search had found the remains of a crashed aircraft (not the Serov An-2R), the remains of a crashed helicopter, and a man wearing few clothes found wandering in the Taiga in a hallucinating and emaciated state, who died of pneumonia in hospital before anyone could find out what had happened to him. This has inevitably led to speculation that the complete disappearance of the aircraft and its passengers is somehow linked to the deaths of the Dyatlov group and that there may be a supernatural element to the disappearance of the An-2R. An article in *Komsomolskaya Pravda* newspaper dated 13 June 2012 outlined this possibility. Another mysterious element to the story was three radio signals picked up and recorded by radio ham Valenin Degtyarev in Nizhny Tagil. Two were made on 4 September 2012 and the third was made on 5 September 2012 between 1.00 a.m. and 3.00 a.m. All were made on the frequency 96.00FM. The signals were weak and it was a rarely used frequency. The transcript of the last message was:

Help! 120 degrees 14 minutes ... bears will eat us up! 120 kilometres from Serov on straight line ... it's all empty, no cartridges. Apply to investigative committee. Help bears will eat up ... help us. 120 kilometres from Serov. 120 thousandth ... upon my soul ... us ... help. Two are wounded. If you don't come that will be the end! Daughter will testify ... knows where ... had been ... the Cossack Ataman was here ... nobody's looking for us. Pothunters, they saw us ... Father, pray for us, hear ... 0 degrees 13.9.7 ... hungry bears will eat up.

It was not known, at the time, if these messages were a hoax. However, the possible links with the deaths of the Dyatlov group, although pure speculation, continued to be promoted by some of the media and various commentators. This was finally laid to rest on Saturday 6 May 2013, when two grouse hunters came across the wreckage (in swampland) of the AN-2R only 8km (5 miles) from Serov airport.

Status of investigation in 2012

The official conclusion in 2012 is still the same as it was in May 1959. The lead criminal investigator on the case, Lev Ivanov, died in the 1990s. After the conclusion of the case on 28 May 1959, he was promoted to Prosecutor in the Kostanai (then spelt Kustanai) Oblast in the Kazakh SSR (now Kazakhstan). He retired in the 1980s and worked for some time in Kostanai as a barrister. Ivanov held his personal belief to the end that the Dyatlov group had all died as a result of UFOs. In 1992 he wrote a letter in which he categorically stated that the cause of the deaths was a UFO.

There are numerous theories as to what happened to the group, with more theories and sub-theories arising all the time. An exchange of letters between the Dyatlov Memorial Foundation and the Russian Federal Security Service (FSB, formerly the KGB) in 2012 asking if they were holding any files or information and suggesting swapping of information (and also requesting a meeting) was met with a very firm rebuttal. The view of the FSB is that the case had been investigated and a conclusion reached, which as far as they are concerned is the end of the matter and the case is closed. This view, however, is not shared by anybody who has looked closely at the case. It is quite apparent that there are far too many anomalies and loose ends for the case to be considered 'concluded' by even the most unenquiring mind. This is not to say that the FSB do actually hold vital information or even take a view on these events (other than their official response to the Dyatlov Memorial Foundation). However, unless there is a change of mind within the FSB, it will never be known whether they have anything that may shed light on the mystery.

Cemeteries

Seven of the group are buried in a row in front of a large memorial (which bears the photographs of all nine) in Mikhailovskoe Cemetery in Ekaterinburg. When they were buried, the plot was open to the street but a high wall was built around the cemetery and although the graves and the memorial are almost directly in front of a gate from the street, the gate is generally locked and you have to go to one of the main entrances and make your way up through the centre of the cemetery. In general, the cemetery is very poorly kept. In summer, areas of it are virtually impossible to get through because of the undergrowth. Many of the graves are almost impossible to see because of the high grass, bushes and trees. More disconcertingly, some bones from some of the graves have come to the surface and present a very unpleasant aspect to the place, quite apart from the disrespect to the memory of the deceased.

The main keeper of the Dyatlov group memory (Yury Kuntsevich of the Dyatlov Memorial Foundation) has long felt that the remains of George Krivonischenko and Semyon Zolotarev should be laid to rest alongside their friends in Mikhailovskoe Cemetery. There are actually eight graves in a row in front of the memorial to the group in Mikhailovskoe Cemetery. Seven of them are occupied by the Dyatlov group, while the eighth grave belongs to another student, Victor Nikitin, who was also from UPI but was nothing whatsoever to do with the group. He had died of pneumonia around the same time, and as eight graves had been prepared in front of the memorial and only seven used by the Dyatlov group, it was decided by the authorities that the eighth plot should be utilised preferably by someone from the same university who was recently deceased.

About 3 miles (5km) away on the other side of the city centre of Ekaterinburg lies Ivanovskoye Cemetery, where both George Krivonischenko and Semyon Zolotarev are buried very close to each other. Ivanovskoye Cemetery is as dilapidated as Mikhailovskoe, with very thick undergrowth in the summer, along with rubbish and empty beer bottles strewn around. Krivonischenko's grave is surrounded by a fenced enclosure with a gate. Both graves lie not far from the footpath near the entrance to the cemetery on Radishcheva Street. Zolotarev's grave is a simple affair with the surround enclosed in concrete and brickwork. In 2012 Yury Kuntsevich of the Dyatlov Memorial Foundation made a request to the relatives of both Krivonischenko and Zolotarev that the graves be disinterred and transferred to Mikhailovskoe Cemetery. The relatives have unfortunately refused to give their permission. It was debated whether to remove some of the soil near both graves and transfer it to the Dyatlov memorial in Mikhailovskoe Cemetery, so that they would all be together finally, at least in spirit. However, the Dyatlov Memorial Foundation has instead arranged to move the headstone of Victor Nikitin, in Mikhailovskoe Cemetery, about 3m away to make room for two more slabs within the memorial area, which will be for Semyon Zolotarev and George Krivonischenko.

There was one final issue being considered in 2012 and that was the possible disinterring of the grave of Semyon Zolotarev, as a number of people, including his sister, did not feel that it was his body that had been buried. This disinterment can be carried out against the wishes of the relatives if any organisation (as opposed to a private individual) makes an application stating their reasons for the disinterment – and provided that the city authority is satisfied with the reasons and issues a permit for the disinterment to go ahead. The remains afterwards must be cremated and not reburied.

Shimon Davidenko

On 20 March 2003 an article appeared in *Evreiskii Kamerton* newspaper under the heading 'Investigation – Death at the Pass'.

The article contained the story of Shimon Davidenko. Davidenko described himself as having lived in Israel for the previous twenty years but prior to that he had lived in Sverdlovsk (Ekaterinburg). His story was that in 1958 he entered the Ural Polytechnic Institute and he immediately signed up to Igor Dyatlov's tourist group. Dyatlov was four years older than Davidenko and he had a far greater experience of hikes of different categories of difficulty (including the highest levels). In autumn 1958 Davidenko joined a group led by Igor Dyatlov that made a hike to the crest of Kholat Syakhl, or 'height 1079', as it was marked on the topographic maps at the time. This hike took place in the November holidays, which was the weekend of 7 November, to celebrate the great October socialist revolution. The group consisted of ten people, including Igor Dyatlov as the leader and also Davidenko. On this trip they walked along the edge of the pass and Mount Otorten and found a good route to the top. However, it started snowing heavily and as the group considered they had reached their objective, they turned back.

Davidenko then goes on to say that on 31 January 1959, Igor Dyatlov set out again for Kholat Syakhl and no one came back. Rescuers who searched the slopes for the lost tourists over a period of several days found nine dead bodies but, the article states, no one was looking for the tenth member of the group, which was himself. It was generally believed that he had not been on that hike. This was because in the middle of January, after he had failed at the Sopromat exam (a very difficult technical subject on the strength of materials), he caught pneumonia as the student vacation began and went to stay with his grandmother, Valentina, in the village of Okvoki in order to recuperate.

As Davidenko's article continues, he describes what he learned about the incident from the accounts of rescuers, the identification protocols and by talking to journalists of *Uralsky Rabochy* (*Urals Worker*), who had not been allowed to publish a word about the tragedy at the pass. The article goes on to describe the group setting up their tent on the slope of Kholat Syakhl before proceeding the following day. He describes the strong wind and snow on that day and says the blue edge of the wood could be seen 1.5km below them. He also describes the search for the missing group and what they found.

He claims in the article that former Sverdlovsk residents living today in Israel or the USA would not disagree with him when he says that the rumours circulating in Sverdlovsk at the time were fantastic. Among the rumours was one that the Dyatlov group had been ritually killed by Voguls (an ancient people related to the Mansi) who lived in the area of the pass. Another rumour was that aliens had appeared in front of them and looked so horrible that it drove them all mad. The third rumour, the one that he said he found most likely, was the testing of a new type of weapon in the area of the pass, related to the testing of a similar weapon at the Novaya Zemlya test field, which was an island over 620 miles (1,000km) to the north in the Polar region.

He states that shortly before his repatriation to Israel in 1990, he spoke to Stanislav Bogomolov, a correspondent of *Uralsky Rabochy* at that time. Bogomolov told him that in the late

1950s work on the design of the first cruise missiles started in the USSR. Bogomolov had only learned this recently at the time, from the *Tekhnika-Molodezhi* (*Technology for the Young*) magazine. In the late 1950s, manufacture of gyro-integrators, or co-ordinate finders for missiles, were being carried out at an electrical instruments plant in Perm. There is a settlement not far from Perm named Bershet where, in that period, a division of the Strategic Missile Forces was deployed.

Bogomolov felt that these were pertinent factors and he spoke to a former state security officer who had been in the KGB in the 1950s and 1960s. Bogomolov had asked him if he knew of the Dyatlov tragedy. The officer (named Nikolaev) replied that he did. He related that there had been food riots by prisoners north of the Sverdlovsk Oblast in November 1959 (presumably meant to be 1958) and that at the end of January 1959 the *zeks* (criminal prisoners) killed their guards and started moving in the direction of the rail-road. It was a crowd of several hundred and they were well armed. Troops with artillery and tanks were brought up to the railway; fifty *zeks* surrendered and the rest disappeared into the Taiga. A decision was taken to fire cruise missiles on all passes and it was bad luck for the Dyatlov group to be there at that time. The cruise missiles were described by the officer as being fitted with vacuum bombs, the effects of which (as already discussed in Chapter 7) can cause injuries like those found on members of the Dyatlov group.

Davidenko confirms in his article that a prisoners' insurgency did take place in the autumn of 1959 (again, presumably he means 1958) and that *zeks* (criminal prisoners) escaped. He again mentions that 'Dyatlov and his people'[5] died not only from hypothermia but also from internal injuries and the 'look of horror on all faces was also a fact that could not be ignored'.[6]

Davidenko then goes on to describe the effect of the power of a vacuum bomb covering an area of several hundred square metres, leaving practically nothing. He stated that such a bomb exploding close to the Dyatlov's tent would have left nothing and they would have been unable to crawl away. He then asks a number of questions: what caused the redness in their eyes? What caused the strange colouring on their faces? Why had the snow around the tent stayed untouched? What must have been the concentration of missile fire to cover the whole of the pass area where the *zeks* were supposedly hiding? Why were no other traces of vacuum blasts around? Finally, where are those hundreds of dead bodies of the escaped *zeks* on whom the missile attack was made?

He then says that all the foregoing was nonsense and gives his own version. He says that the correspondents in the winter of 1959 who were trying to understand the causes of the tragedy had omitted one fact that was, however, mentioned in the materials of the investigation case. Dyatlov's group went to the pass carrying with them a ten-person tent and a full outfit and supply of food for ten people. Rescuers found nine bodies. Investigators came to the conclusion that there were nine members of the expedition, and all of them died. The tenth one should have been Davidenko, but he had fallen ill and could not join the Dyatlov group – and so stayed alive.

In February 1959 he was summoned to the prosecutor's office three times, and Investigator Lev Ivanov persistently questioned him[7] about how it happened that he had been so lucky, and what he knew about the dead student's personalities. Ivanov seemed to be quite satisfied with a UFO version of the deaths and did not take the trouble to find out whether Davidenko had really spent those days with his grandmother in the village.

Yet Davidenko says he had not been with his grandmother. On the evening of 30 January 1959 he ran away from his 'poor old granny' and joined the Dyatlov group right before they went on the hike. He says the group were expecting him and accordingly were carrying a complete outfit and equipment for ten people. He had agreed everything with Igor Dyatlov on the phone and had not the least desire to drink fresh warm milk by the stove while the group would have been ascending Kholat Syakhl.

Davidenko says he was with the group on that night at the pass and he was the only one who stayed alive. For thirty-six years, he says, he kept silent about what he had witnessed. What he has read over the years about the incident, he describes as an amount of fiction and nonsense that exceeds all limits. The memory of his comrades, he says, which he felt was being played with like a long-forgotten toy, is the reason he could not keep silent any longer.

The following is quoted in his own (translated) words:

On the night of 2 February we reached the edge of the pass and set up a tent. Igor Dyatlov and Natasha Kolmogorova made dinner, we sang songs to a guitar and went to sleep at about midnight. The weather was fine, the sky was cloudy, it snowed slightly, the calm air and frost were bracing, and we felt very warm in the tent.

I woke up at 1.30 a.m. because it seemed to me that I heard some howling at a distance. I listened and decided that it was the rising wind and I was hearing its gusts. Wind could destroy our plans, so I got dressed, left the tent and laced up the entrance to keep the warm air inside.

There was no wind, and it had stopped snowing. The howling came from the side of the forest, from the ravine below. I felt my hair stand on end under the cap. Truly, it was that raising feeling of horror of which investigator Ivanov spoke later. I wanted to run, no matter where, just run away as far as possible.

All was quiet in the tent, the tourists slept. I managed to take control of myself. I was trembling, and slowly started moving down to the ravine, where the group's dead bodies would later be found. The howling was getting louder, the feeling of horror was rising, but it was that feeling from which, in theory, I should have run away from as fast as I could, but it was drawing me down, towards its source.

Can you imagine the situation? Something terrible awaits you in a black room, but you go exactly there and are unable to do anything about it.

I remember vaguely what happened next. I think I was saved because I was warmly dressed and I also found chocolate in the pocket of my overalls, which I instinctively put in my mouth. I think I was the only one at the pass on that night who had been properly dressed and the only one who had some food. Igor Dyatlov with the others, in horror, jumped out of their sleeping bags into the cold, and this killed them. There were several hundred *zeks* at the pass on that night, they were poorly clothed and hungry and that killed them, too. The lower in the ravine, the stronger was the horror that, like the frost, seized my mind. I forgot absolutely about the others I had left on the slope. I was only looking ahead, and at some moment saw a group of people. They were howling in horrifying voices and stripping off their clothes. One of them fell down, but nobody stopped. Then another one fell down, and one more …

I remember how I stepped over a body, and how I ran after those screaming and howling people. I only remember for sure that I myself ran in silence and chewed chocolate while running. I never liked chocolate before, but this time I could not resist it, and put lump after lump in my mouth.

It was probably an instinct of self-preservation, which knows better than your mind what one must do.

Then I completely stopped thinking what was happening around me.[8]

Davidenko then says he came to his senses in the morning and was dragging himself along a road. He saw a farmstead ahead of him. He knocked on the door and asked where he was and was told Korobeiniki, which Davidenko says was 4 miles (7km) south of their route. From Korobeiniki he went to Bitnoye where he took a bus to Perm with the little money he had and was back at his grandmother's village the following day. He told no one about what had happened and surmised that neither vacuum bombs nor cruise missiles had been used to kill the *zeks*, but he says it was most likely a nerve gas of neuroparalytic action. His opinion was that before it took effect, the gas would allow someone to continue for a distance, as the members of the Dyatlov group had, moving down the slope from the tent. His opinion of the serious internal injuries suffered by Luda Dubinina, Semyon Zolotarev and Nicolai Thibeaux-Brignolle is that it was misinformation 'leaked' by the Prosecutor's Office and he asks if anyone has seen the autopsy reports.

After that night, he says that a reddish sheen appeared in his eyes but that the colour of his skin did not change, otherwise the watchful investigator Ivanov would never have let go of him and he would not have got to Israel.

Davidenko's article also appeared on an Internet forum where the responses in the comments were very negative and critical to the extent that some are unprintable.

There are numerous anomalies in Davidenko's, it has to be said, quite fantastic account.

There is no mention of Yury Yudin, who was the tenth member of the group. The start date of the expedition was

23 January not 31 January. The searcher he names in his article as Latyshev is an unknown name. The early stages of the search did not take three weeks, as he claims, and they were not held up by snow. The Dyatlov group had no sleeping bags, only blankets. The front of the tent was buttoned not laced. The guitar is a mandolin.

He talks of Natasha Kolmogorova in his article rather than Zinaida Kolmogorova, and there was no official mention anywhere of her blood staining the snow near her mouth, as Davidenko states. His statement that 'According to the rescuers, the faces of all the dead had an expression of horror',[9] is probably journalistic licence, as most of the bodies were in a state of semi-decomposition and no expressions could be made out. His statement that the eyes of all the dead had a reddish colour is not mentioned anywhere else, and also the eyes of some of the bodies were actually missing when found. Okvoki village is not mentioned on present-day maps, which is not to say it has not been absorbed into a larger settlement. Korobeiniki is south of Perm, but Perm itself is almost 300 miles (490km) from the pass and Kholat Syakhl. Bitnoye is several kilometres north of Perm, but would have been impossible to be reached by foot in one day from the pass.

There was a rail-based Mobile Rocket Division based at Bershet but it was not formed until 1970. The Soviet Strategic Rocket Forces itself was not formed until 17 December 1959, over eight months after the deaths took place. Although the rocket forces were being developed prior to the formation of the Strategic Rocket Forces as a separate military arm, the possibility that strategic or even tactical rockets would be fired at a group of escaped prisoners in the mountains 335 miles (540km) away is fanciful to say the least.

Visiting the Dyatlov Pass

A visitor making a trip to the present-day Dyatlov Pass would have to spend some time and money in preparing for it. He or she would also need to have a certain degree of fitness as it is best to make the last part of the journey by foot, although for the well-heeled it is possible to fly there by helicopter (though very expensive) from Uktus general aviation airport 3 miles (5km) south of the main Koltsovo Airport for Ekaterinburg. It is also possible to go in a four-wheel drive vehicle and a number of adventurous types have done this, but it can be a difficult journey – some experienced hikers say it is possible to pass these vehicles on foot, so slow can be the going due to the condition of the muddy and waterlogged ground in the initial stages of some of the route the Dyatlov group took along the Auspia and Lozva rivers (or the route further north depending on whether you support the official or unofficial versions of the story). A number of tour groups and guides offer accompanied trips to the Dyatlov Pass with an English-speaking guide. These are not cheap (around 26,500 rubles per person as at summer 2012) and they usually require a group of around eight or more people. Yury Kuntsevich of the Dyatlov Memorial Foundation regularly makes trips to the Dyatlov Pass from Ekaterinburg accompanying both individuals and groups and it is highly recommended to make the journey in his company. Apart from his unsurpassed knowledge of the Dyatlov tragedy, he is also very knowledgeable on the ways of the Mansi and he generally takes groups along Mansi trails and meets with Mansi hunters.

Conclusion

Probably what happened on the night of 1/2 February 1959 will never be actually known. Each theory of what happened to the Dyatlov group has its own adherents with no overall majority for one particular theory. Perhaps the answer is a mixture of more than one theory. There is, however, a fairly overwhelming agreement among the theorists that, whatever theory they hold, there has been an official cover-up of some kind.

The official attitude towards accidents involving the military in the Soviet Union is best illustrated by what happened in 1979 in the same city where twenty years earlier the Dyatlov group set out from – Sverdlovsk. On Friday 30 March 1979 a worker in Military Compound-19 in the south-west of the city took an air filter off a piece of drying machinery in order to clean it as it was clogged, and left a note for his supervisor informing him that he had done so. The supervisor did not see the note and therefore did not make an entry in the logbook as he should have done. The supervisor of the next shift arrived on Monday 2 April 1979, and not seeing anything in the logbook, started up the machinery. The result was the release of deadly anthrax spores in an aerosol form into the open atmosphere between 1.30 p.m. and 4 p.m. that day. Military Compound-19 and its associated Military Compound-32 in Sverdlovsk was a microbiological warfare research establishment containing 5,000 people (Military Compound-32 contained a further 10,000 people). The anthrax was the most virulent strain known as 'anthrax 836', which among other uses was intended to be fitted to the warheads of SS-18 ICBMs targeted on cities in the USA. The air filter was found and put back on and the accident reported to the local military command, but was not immediately reported to the local city authorities. Had the wind been going in the opposite direction, the spores would have gone into the city of 1.2 million people. As it was, the wind carried the spores in a south-east direction into the countryside.

Nevertheless, there were a number of deaths. Workers in a nearby ceramic plant were given pills to take but many were dead within a week. The total number of people who died will probably never be known but it is estimated at least sixty-five deaths. All medical files and records in local hospitals associated with the patients were confiscated by the KGB. The official announcement by the authorities was that contaminated meat sold by local butchers was responsible for the deaths. When livestock in six villages lying southeast of Military Compound-19 died from anthrax, this was given as proof of the source of the outbreak. There was deep concern in the West, not least that the USSR was breaking the terms of the 1972 Microbiological Warfare Convention by continuing research in this area. Despite assurances given by Soviet physicians, including a visit to the USA to give a presentation, it was to be 1992 before a Western team led by Professor Matthew Meselson of Harvard University arrived in what was now Ekaterinburg to investigate.[12] Professor Meselson had accepted the original story of contaminated meat, but his investigations in 1992 left no room for doubt of a military accident – and this was without access to the medical files of the deceased, which had been confiscated by the KGB. It is believed that all the medical records and any associated evidence were destroyed by the KGB.

Involved in the cover-up was the future Russian premier Boris Yeltsin, who was the local Communist Party boss at the time and, coincidentally, a graduate of the same university as the Dyatlov group – UPI.

No journalist has been allowed on the site since 1992 and the site is still heavily guarded by troops with dogs, although all work of this nature was moved to underground facilities.

There are similarities with the Dyatlov group deaths. Perhaps the most overwhelming similarity between the two cases is that the authorities are not giving the full story and in both cases there is possible military involvement. There is also KGB involvement in both cases, with the existence of 'a secret file'. The KGB files in the anthrax case were destroyed in 1990 by order of the Council of Ministers.

While the investigations into the anthrax case by Professor Meselson and his team have virtually proven military involvement, despite the denials of the Russian authorities, the same cannot be said in the Dyatlov case. At the very least, the general feeling is that the authorities have not released all the facts of the Dyatlov case. The final 'official' report into the matter consists of two thick files and it concludes that the Dyatlov incident was 'not a man-made disaster'.[10] This is a term that can be interpreted in a number of ways, including an act of God or the supernatural. Coupled with the term from the autopsies of 'an unknown compelling force'[11] killing some of the group, it is a most unsatisfactory conclusion.

There is also the question of another case file, Case No. 3/2518–59 (see Chapter 7), which the authorities will not release.

Despite the despatch of four experts from Moscow, the presence of so many senior civil and particularly military officials in Ivdel during the period of the search raises the question: why? Why in particular would one or more military officers of the rank of general be involved in what was basically at that stage a search for lost skiers, and civil ones at that? At the near height of the Cold War, one would have expected military generals to be concerning themselves with planning to fight a potential war against their capitalist foes in NATO rather than supervising a search for missing skiers in a provincial backwater. Even if help was requested from the military by the civil authorities (in addition to a civil Mi-8, two military Mi-8 helicopters also took part in the operations), it would have been expected that a general would have let someone further down the pecking order concern himself with the detail and involvement in the search itself. The conclusion that must be drawn from all this is that the deaths of the Dyatlov group were, in all probability, due to some kind of an accident caused by the military.

The tenth member of the Dyatlov group, Yury Yudin, who saved his life by turning around because of illness, sadly passed away on 27 April 2013. He spent his retirement living in Solikamsk, a city 200km north or Perm, and assisting wherever he could in maintaining the memory of the Dyatlov group through the Dyatlov Foundation. He was finally reunited with his friends in the Mikhailovskoe Cemetery on 4 May 2013.

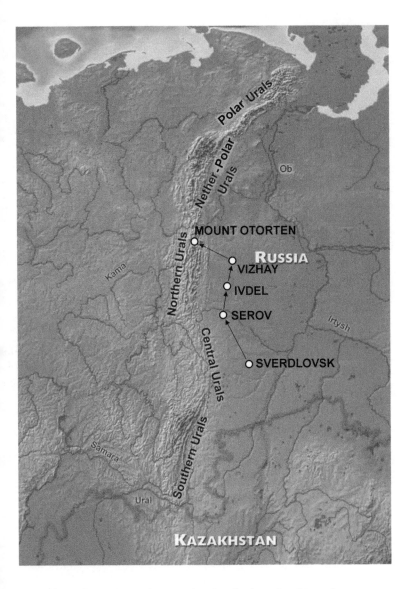

1 Route taken by the Dyatlov group from Sverdlovsk, north to Mount Otorten.
Leah Monahan

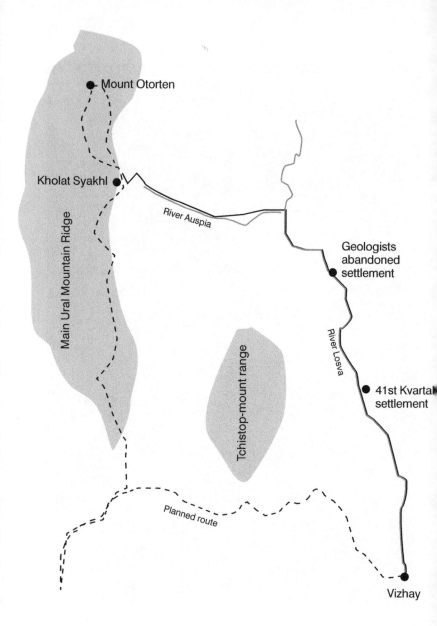

2 Route taken from Vizhay to the woodcutters' settlement (41st Kvartal), the abandoned geologist settlement and Kholat Syakhl.

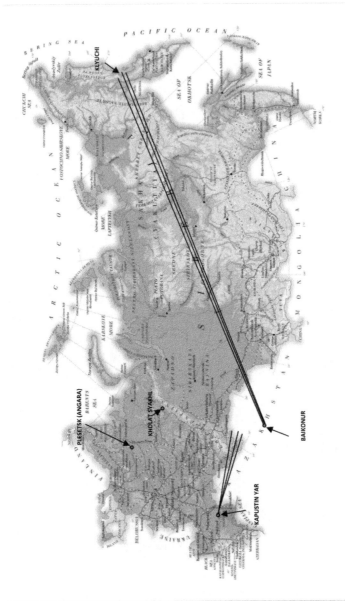

the lanes from Baikonur to the impact area at Klyuchi on the Kamchatka Peninsula.
Leah Monahan

205

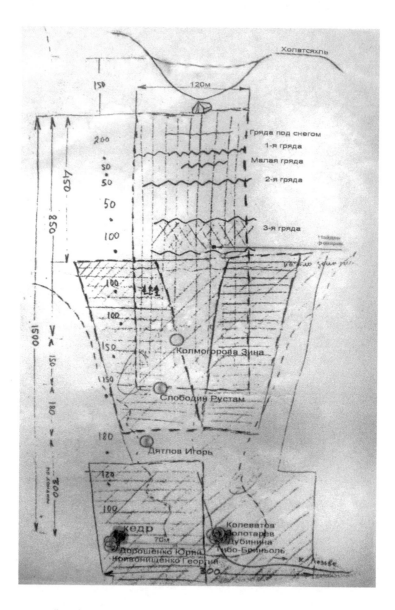

4 A chart drawn by one of the search party of the locations of the tent, the bodies and the search areas. *Courtesy Dyatlov Memorial Foundation*

Appendix I

Timeline

1959

23 Jan   Full party of ten leave Sverdlovsk railway station to Serov. An eleventh member of the group is too late and fails to reach the railway station in time for the departure. He decides not to try and catch up with the group and thus saves his life.

24 Jan   Group arrive in Serov. George Krivonischenko is arrested by the police for creating a disturbance at Serov railway station.

24–25 Jan   Group arrives at Ivdel railway station just after midnight and wait there for transport to Vizhay the following morning.

25 Jan   The group travel from Ivdel to Vizhay by bus where they spend the night of 25/26 January in very basic accommodation.

26 Jan   They leave Vizhay at 1.10 p.m. on an open GAZ-63 truck to travel to 41st Kvartal (woodcutters settlement).

27 Jan   After spending the night at the 41st Kvartal settlement, they leave for the second severny (an abandoned village of around twenty huts) using a borrowed horse and cart to take their packs. They spend the night of 27/28 January in one of the huts.

28 Jan   Yury Yudin decides to turn back and return to Sverdlovsk on account of the severe pain in his back and leg.

30 Jan   The group move along the River Auspia, a right-hand tributary of the River Lozva, following the sleigh-and-deer track on the riverbank. Midway they reach an old Mansi camp. The deer path ends and they continue moving across virgin snow, which is hard work because the snow is almost 120cm deep.

31 Jan   Last entry is made in the diary by Igor Dyatlov.

1 Feb	Tent is pitched just before sunset. At some point, believed to be approximately two to three hours after the tent is pitched, something happens forcing the group to exit the tent as fast as possible by slashing their way out of it.
26 Feb	The tent is discovered by Boris Slobtsov and his search party.
27 Feb	First bodies found by cedar tree – George Krivonischenko and Yury Doroshenko. This was quickly followed by discovery of Igor Dyatlov's body 400m from the cedar tree and then the discovery of the body of Zina Kolmogorova 500m away from the cedar tree.
5 March	Body of Rustem Slobodin is found.
3–5 May	Remaining bodies (Luda Dubinina, Alexander Kolevatov, Semyon Zolotarev, Nicolai Thibeaux-Brignolle) are found by a den they had tried to create to protect themselves from the severe weather.

Appendix II

Radiation Analysis Report

Extract

Samples of solid biosubstrates and clothes combined in groups under Nos
1, 2, 3, 4 were submitted to the radio-isotope laboratory of the Sverdlovsk
sanitary-epidemic station and were analyzed for presence of radioactive
materials.

Dosimetric measurements of clothes showed excessive radioactivity
(Beta-emission only, no Alpha or Gamma-quanta) of 200–300 counts per
minute (cpm) over the natural background. Further investigation allowed
maximum contamination to be established on different spots
of clothing:

Brown sweater from No. 4: 9900 cpm on 150 sq.cm.
Bottom part of bloomers from No. 1: 5000 cpm on 150 sq.cm.
Belt of sweater from No. 1: 5600 cpm on 150 sq.cm.

Table 1. Contamination on different items of clothing. The underlined figures
show higher than expected levels of radiation due to contamination. Test

washing in cold running water during three hours showed 30–60 per cent contamination removal.

	Name	Area, sq.cm	Total cpm	Radioactivity of contaminated spot	Radioactivity of contaminated spot in terms of 150 sq.cm
1	Soil from No. 1	-	96	-	-
2	Belt of sweater from No. 1	70	384	9600	5600
			300		
	After washing		244		2700
			218		
3	Bottom part of bloomers from No. 1	55	297	1840	5000
			265		
	After washing		210	970	2600
			184		
4	Oт No.2	60	182	820	2000
			160		
	After washing		182	560	1400
			163		
5	Sheepskin, jacket	60	176	770	1920
	After washing		156	370	940
6	Bottom part of trousers from No. 3	66	120	1070	1800
	After washing		111	100	230
7	Jacket from No. 4	88	210	1070	1800
	After washing		177	690	1160
8	Black leggings from No. 4	77	164	660	1280
	After washing		140	360	700
9	White sweater from No. 4	63	185	850	1840
	After washing		163	560	1340
10	Brown sweater from No. 4	75	640	4900	9900
			390	2600	5200

Table 2. Radiometric measurements of samples of solid biosubstrate from Nos 1, 2, 3, 4. These are tissues from the Dyatlov group bodies. The radiation readings were within the norm. The underlined 8400 is within the norm and due to the natuaral presence of radioactive isotope K^{40} in human tissue.

	Name	Sample mass, g	Raw sample mass, g	Ash mass, g	Background count	Excess over background	Sample activity, cmp	Sample activity, curie/kg
1	Intestines, No. 1	0.2	24.42	0.670	23	3	2000	0.9×10^{-9}
2	Liver, No. 1	0.2	19.130	0.690	22	3	3000	1.35×10^{-9}
3	Brain, No. 1	0.2	42.820	0.710	26	4	1850	0.85×10^{-9}
4	Heart, No. 1	0.2	8.500	1300	24	2	<u>8400</u>	3.8×10^{-9}
5	Skin, No. 1	0.25	1.400	0.025	24	-	-	-
6	Intestines, No.2	0.2	20.47	0.350	23	6	2800	1.25×10^{-9}
7	Liver, No. 2	0.2	13.59	0.480	29	6	5800	2.6×10^{-9}
8	Brain, No. 2	0.2	41.00	0.840	26	4	2200	1×10^{-9}
9	Stomach, No. 2	0.2	24.400	0.480	29	3	1600	0.85×10^{-9}
10	Breastbone, No. 2	0.2	4.170	0.740	24	-	-	-
11	Breastbone, rib, No. 2	0.2	4.300	0.390	24	-	-	-
12	Skin of thigh, No. 2	0.022	6.500	0.300	24	-	-	-
13	Intestines, No. 3	0.3	21.770	0.740	23	3	2800	1.25×10^{-9}
14	Liver, No. 3	0.2	33.00	0.920	20	6	4600	2×10^{-9}
15	Kidney, No. 3	0.08	10.10	0.080	26	-	-	-
16	Skin, No. 3	0.014	1.150	0.040	24	-	-	-
17	Breastbone, No. 3	0.2	7.200	1.300	24	-	-	-
18	Intestines, No. 4	0.058	14.10	0.100	23			
19	Liver, No. 4	0.2	18.830	0.490	34	7	5000	2.2×10^{-9}
20	Kidneys, No. 4	0.2	18.470	0.330	27	4	2000	0.9×10^{-9}
21	Skin, No. 4	0.091	11.910	0.100	27	4	900	0.6×10^{-9}
22	Skin of thigh, No. 4	0.2	7.600	0.280	24	2	2000	0.9×10^{-9}
23	Skin of shin, No. 4	0.1	3.840	9.150	24	-	-	-
24	Heart, No. 4	0.2	10.720	0.350	24	4	3000	1.4×10^{-9}
25	Rib, No. 4	0.177	1.300	0.180	24	-	-	-

Table 3. Check sample measurements (tissues of a person killed in a street accident, provided for comparison by forensic medical expert Dr Vozrozhdenny)

	Name	Sample mass, g	Raw sample mass, g	Ash mass, g	Background count	Excess over background	Sample activity, cmp	Sample activity, curie/kg
1	Lung	0.2	23.100	0.700	24	+3	2500	1.1×10^{-9}
2	Kidney	0.2	30.200	0.920	24	+1	-	-
3	Liver	0.2	26.030	0.960	24	+1	-	-
4	Heart	0.2	19.640	0.950	24	+1	8000	3.6×10^{-9}
5	Skin	0.25	28.200	0.690	24	+6	2000	0.9×10^{-9}
6	Rib	0.2	13.800	1.180	24	+2	4700	2.1×10^{-9}

The investigation results shown in Tables 2 and 3 show no excess over average content of radioactive materials in human tissues.

Conclusions:

The content of radioactive materials in analyzed solid biosubstartes is within the natural level (and is due to the presence of isotope K-40).

The analyzed samples of clothing carry slightly excessive amounts of radioactive substances being the source of Beta-emission.

The detected radioactive materials or radioactive substance show a tendency to washing-off in the course of clothing samples washing, i.e., they are not due to a neutron flux or induced radiation, but rather to radioactive contamination with Beta-particles.

Chief Radiologist Levashov

27.05.59

Appendix III

'Light Set' guidelines

As taken from the translated article on www.Russia-paramormal.org.

Observations by Yury Yakimov (in his own words) on the operations of the 'light set' he encountered and believes responsible for the Dyatlov group deaths (see Chapter 8).

Based on the observations made by V. Rudkovsky (forest ranger) and myself, some conclusions may be made:

1. The 'light set' makes its appearance after dark, in complete silence, emits light for four to four and a half hours and leaves with a noise resembling strong electric discharge (snapping). After the light is gone, a strong wind blows for two to three minutes.
2. The light emitted by the 'set' resembles that of a projector, like from halogen or neon lamps.
3. The light from the 'set' may oscillate vertically, go in different directions and change direction.
4. The source of the light may be located on or above the ground surface.
5. The 'light set' responds to human glance (or maybe to animal glance as well). From the source of light, torches separate and quickly move towards a person as if catching a human glance.
6. The light of the torches dazzles a person, like headlights or strong spot-light.
7. The light casts no shade from trees.
8. Torches may pass through the forest, dividing and swinging. Their number increases from two to eight.
9. The 'set' does not respond to turned-on electric lamp KC-2000.
10. The 'set' does not respond to fire or a glowing cigarette.
11. The 'set' does not respond to a human voice.
12. The 'set' does not respond to sound of a car.
13. The 'set' may appear at any time of the year and in any weather.
14. The 'set' does not respond to human thermal energy, only to a glance.

If we adopt the version that the Dyatlov group met with a similar phenomenon on that tragic night, one more conclusion may be made:

15. The 'set' displays aggression against man.

The 'set' is tuned to protect information from man. In case of a long glance
on this phenomenon, a beam of light is sent from the source, it lights a
person. Torches separate from the light source, they try to locate the human
glance with their beams. They approach and getting closer than 50m they
may send some narrow-focused shock wave aiming at a human glance,
which may inflict severe injuries. It may be not just a shock wave, but a
high-power infrasonic wave at 7–8Hz frequency, which may cause the feeling of panic in humans.

Probably there are other people who had seen such a phenomenon and
can give more information about the 'light set'. It leaves some negative psy-
chological after-effect in a person who has watched it.

Notes

Chapter 1

The bulk of this chapter is constructed from the group diary for the period of their journey along with comments made by the sole survivor, Yury Yudin.

1. Dyatlov group diary extract.
2. Dyatlov group diary extract.
3. The nuclear accident that happened in 1958 in which Krivonischenko took part in rescue operations actually took place at a closed city known as Chelyabinsk 40, not far from Kyshtym, but it is referred to as the Kyshtym Accident or Incident.
4. See *The Decryption of a Picture* by Henry S. Lowenhaupt (declassified CIA files available on the Internet) – a fascinating account of how information was extracted from a single photograph in the July 1958 issue of Russian magazine *Oganek* on how power was supplied to atomic facilities in the Urals. The picture showed the Sverdlovsk Central Despatching Office of the Urals Electric Power System. Charles V. Reeves (working for the CIA's nuclear energy power division) was able over a period of time to work out the power consumed by the plants from diagrams on a board in the photograph www.cia.gov/library.
5. See *The Decryption of a Picture* by Henry S. Lowenhaupt www.cia.gov/library.
6. Details from Wikipedia http://en.wikipedia.org/ivdel.
7. It is possible that some of the 'workers' they described are actually workers from the Ivdel camp system, i.e. Gulag prisoners, but there is no mention in the diary.
8. Illegal songs may have been sung by ex-Gulag prisoners present at the camp.
9. Article 58 of the Soviet Penal Code introduced the notion of an 'enemy of the worker' as opposed to an 'enemy of the people'. The Dyatlov group were, strictly speaking, in contravention of Section 12 of the code, which

allowed for the arrest and prosecution of any onlookers who failed to report instances of anyone contravening Section 10 of the code. Section 10 allowed for the arrest and prosecution of anyone indulging in 'propaganda or agitation against the Soviet Union'. Article 58 was extensively rewritten after Khrushchev's denunciation of Stalin.

Chapter 2

1. There is some dispute over when and where the M-4 Bisons were observed. Some state it was Aviation Day at Tushino Airfield, near Moscow in July 1955, although others say it took place at the May Day Parade in the same year.
2. *Kitchen Debate* http://en.wikipedia.org/wiki/Kitchen_Debate.
3. Ibid.

Chapter 3

The bulk of the chapter has been provided by information from the staff of the Spring Day Museum at URFU (formerly UPI) and the book *Sport in Soviet Society* by James Riordan, Cambridge University Press (1977). Based on the author's thesis (University of Birmingham), this is probably the most comprehensive description of how sport fitted into Soviet society, starting in 1861 and covering up to 1975.

1. From the famoud Latin quotation *Mens saba in corpore sana.*

Chapter 4

1. Much of the background information on Semyon Zolotarev has been provided by the Dyatlov Memorial Foundation.
2. Exhortations used by authorities to workers and military personnel to spur them on to greater efforts. The references to Stalin continued for some time after his death.
3. The Red Book of the Peoples of the Russian Empire www.eki.ee/books/redbook/mansis.shtml.
4. Ibid.
5. See *The Mansi – History and Present Day*, Aado Lintrop, Institute of the Estonian Language http://folklore.ee/~aado/rahvad/mansingl.htm.
6. The Red Book of the Peoples of the Russian Empire www.eki.ee/books/redbook/mansis.shtml.
7. Ibid.

Chapter 5

The bulk of this chapter consists of information provided by the courtesy of the Dyatlov Memorial Foundation.

1. http://en.wikipedia.org/wiki/meninges.

Chapter 6

1. 'Paradoxical Undressing in Fatal Hypothermia', B. Wedin, L. Vangaard and J. Hiroven, *Journal of Forensic Science* 1979, Jul 24 (3): 543–53.
2. 'Terminal Burrowing Behaviour – A Phenomenon of Lethal Hypothermia', M. A. Rothschild and V. Schneider, Institute of Legal Medicine, Freie Universitat Berlin, Germany. In the study of sixty-nine deaths studied between 1978 and 1994, all the bodies were found in a state of undress but additionally were found under a bed, behind a wardrobe and on a shelf. The deceased had made last desperate attempts to seek extra protection from the cold by the 'burrowing behaviour'.
3. 'Terminal Burrowing Behaviour – A Phenomenon of Lethal Hypothermia', M. A. Rothschild and V. Schneider.
4. Wikipedia article for the majority of the details on avalanches: http://en.wikipedia.org/wiki/avalanche.
5. See *The Mystery of the Deaths of the Dyatlov Group*, E. Bujanov and B. Slobtsov, which supports the avalanche theory as being responsible for the deaths.
6. Declassified CIA National Intelligence Estimate Number 11-5-59, Soviet Capabilities in Guided Missiles and Space Vehicles (among numerous other sources and other declassified CIA files available on the Internet).
7. Lists of launches can be found on the website Encyclopedia Astronautica: www.astronautix.com.
8. Details of some of Dr Vladimir Gavreau's work can be found on the Académie française website www.academie-francaise.fr and other details of his work can readily be found on the Internet (although some of it is copyright).
9. Anne Applebaum, *Gulag: A History*, Penguin 2003.
10. Anne Applebaum, *Gulag: A History*.
11. Anne Applebaum, *Gulag: A History*.
12. Anne Applebaum, *Gulag: A History*.
13. http://dinets.travel.ru/russianbears.htm.
14. www.wolfsongalaska.org/wolf_russia_russia_history.html.
15. Philip Mantle and Paul Stonehill hope to publish their research into the 'lair of the golden woman' in 2013.

Chapter 7

1. Based on a theory entitled 'A Fight in the Higher Echelons of Power', Alexander Gulikov (unpublished).
2. Comment taken from the official investigation notes and strogly disputed by Gennady Kisilov.
3. Term used by Gennady Kisilov in his study of the official investigation

papers to describe his scepticism at the official portryal of the Group rushing away from the mountain to their deaths.

4. Term used by Gennady Kisilov in his study of the official investigation papers to describe pieces of twisted cloth used to move the bodies.

5. Ivdel investigator Vladimir Korotayev's derogatory description of the behaviour of the members of the 'Exraordinary Commision for Rescue Operations'.

6. Ivdel investigator Vladimir Korotayev's derogatory description of the purpose of the member of the 'Extraordinary Commission for Rescue Operations', which had been set up to bring a focus to the search, but in Korotayev's view was little more than a talk shop with planty of drinking in the village of Pershino near Ivdel.

Chapter 8

Yury Yakimov's theory is a translated and condensed version of the original on the website www.Russia-paranormal.org.

Chapter 9

1. Ekaterina Loushnikova, *Outcasts – Inmates of the Black Eagle*, 27 October 2010.

2. Ekaterina Loushnikova, *Outcasts – Inmates of the Black Eagle*.

3. Ekaterina Loushnikova, *Outcasts – Inmates of the Black Eagle*.

4. Air Safety Network website for Serov An-2R www.aviation-safety.net.

5. Reference by Shimon Davidenko to the Dyatlov group, in 'Investigation – Death at the Pass', *Evreiskii Kamerton*, 20 March 2003.

6. Davidenko to how the bodies of the Dyatlov group were found, in *ibid*. This assertion was nor borne out by the facts.

7. This claim was made by Davidenko without any suppoting evidence.

8. Davidenko's account in 'Investigation – Death at the Pass', *Evreiskii Kamerton*, 20 March 2003.

9. Davidenko to how the bodies of the Dyatlov group were found, in *ibid*. This assertion was nor borne out by the facts.

10. The conclusion of the official investigation in to the incident led by Lev Ivanov.

11. The conclusion of the authopsies in to the causes of the Dyatlov group deaths; the actual wording was 'elemental force'.

12. Details of the anthrax investigation are given in Jeanne Guillemin, *Anthrax: An investigation of a Deadly Outbreak*, University of California Press, 2001.

Select bibliography

From a research point of view, all roads lead to the Dyatlov Memorial Foundation. The following is useful for background and information; a number of the items mentioned below directly concerning the Dyatlov tragedy have generally been provided by the Dyatlov Memorial Foundation.

Publications in English

Anthrax: An Investigation of a Deadly Outbreak, Jeanne Guillemin, University of California Press 2001

Gulag: A History of the Soviet Camps, Anne Applebaum, Penguin 2003

The Gulag Archipeligo Part 1 & 2, Alexander Solzhenitzyn, 1st ed., Harper Row 1974

Mysterious Sky: Soviet UFO Phenomenon, Philip Mantle and Paul Stonehill, PublishAmerica 2006

One Day in the Life of Ivan Denisovich Alexander Solzhenitzyn, Penguin reprint 2000

'Paradoxical Undressing in Fatal Hypotheria', B. Wedlin, L. Vangaard and J. Hiroven, *Journal of Forensic Science*, 24 (3), July 1919, pp. 543–53

Red Plenty, Francis Spufford, Faber & Faber, 2010

Sport in Soviet Society, James Riordan, Cambridge University Press 1977

Terminal Burrowing Behaviour – A Phenomenon of Lethal Hypothermia, M.A. Rothschild and V. Schneider, Institute of Legal Medicine, Freie Universitat Berlin, Germany 1995

UFO Case Files of Russia, Philip Mantle and Paul Stonehill, Healings of Atlantis Ltd, 2010

Publications in Russian

Death 'Classified', Istina, Tyumen 2012 Oleg Arkhipov

'Investigation – Death at the Pass', *Evreiskii Kamerton*, 20 March 2003

Kaleidoscope, No. 28, 10 July 2006

Teoriya I metodika fizicheskoi kul'tury, G.D. Kharabuga, Moscow 1969

'The Dyatlov Pass', Anna Matveyeva (fiction), *Ural*, No. 1, 2001
'The Mystery of the Deaths of the Dyatlov Group', E. Bujanov and
   B. Slobtsov, *Uralsky Rabochy*, Ekaterinburg 2011
The Price of State Secrets is Nine Lives, Anatoly Guschin, printing house of
   Asbest (city in Sverdlovsk Oblast) 1999

Internet sources
An example of one of the many websites covering the Dyatlov incident is:
   www.forteantimes.com
Gennady Kizilov. Death of Tourists – 1959. Publication on the web: http://
   samlib.ru/k/kizilow_g_i/150308-1.shtml)
Outcasts – Inmates of the Black Eagle, Ekaterina Loushnikova, 27 October
   2010: www.opendemocracy.net
The Decryption of a Picture, Henry S, Lowenhaupt: www.cia.gov/library

Televison
Riddle of the Skies – In Russia (Discovery Channel)

Newspapers
Komsomolskaya Pravda, 13 June 2012
Oblastnaya Gazeta, 30 January 1999

More From the Author
For photos of the author's trip to the Dyatlov Pass, please go to:
http://www.dyatlov-pass-incident.com/

For other books by the author, please go to:
http://www.keithmccloskey.com/

Index

221